Cecilia Mary Caddell

A History of the Missions in Paraguay

Cecilia Mary Caddell

A History of the Missions in Paraguay

ISBN/EAN: 9783743331761

Manufactured in Europe, USA, Canada, Australia, Japa

Cover: Foto ©ninafisch / pixelio.de

Manufactured and distributed by brebook publishing software (www.brebook.com)

Cecilia Mary Caddell

A History of the Missions in Paraguay

CONTENTS.

CHAPTER I.
SPANIARDS AND INDIANS.

Character of the Spanish colonists. The system of *encomienda*. First missionary efforts. Arrival of the Jesuit Fathers. Their labours and successes among the Indians . . . 1

CHAPTER II.
SEARCH FOR SOULS.

The Jesuits oppose the enslaving of the natives. Appeal to the king. Manifesto of the Fathers. Rapacity of the colonists. The first "reductions," and the first martyrs. Renewed contentions. Second appeal to the home government, which supports the Jesuits. Expulsion of the Fathers from Assumption 13

CHAPTER III.
FIRST FOUNDATIONS.

Paraguay. Character and habits of the natives. The work of conversion and civilisation. Description of a reduction. Its internal government. Occupations of the missionaries. Regulations as to property and commerce 27

CHAPTER IV.
A DAY IN THE REDUCTIONS.

Church, schools, workshops, &c. Feast of Corpus Christi. Diversions. Religious and moral habits of the people. Their zeal for the conversion of their brethren. Arrival of fresh missionaries. Ravages of the small-pox . . . 43

CHAPTER V.

THE MAMELUKES OF ST. PAUL'S.

St. Paul's. Lawlessness of its inhabitants. Their treachery and cruelty to the Indians. Attack on the reductions. First migrations. Courage and determination of the missionaries. Crimes of the "Mamelukes." The Fathers resolve to evacuate the reductions 56

CHAPTER VI.

THE RETREAT ON THE PARANA.

Disasters and sufferings of the emigrants. Spaniards continue to molest the old reductions. Flight of the inhabitants. Renewed attacks of the Mamelukes. The Indians, allowed the use of fire-arms, defeat the marauders. New settlements. Intrepidity of the missionaries. Bernardin de Cardenas, Bishop of Assumption. His charges against the Jesuits. The fable of the gold-mines. Insurrection of the colonists quelled by the Christian natives 76

CHAPTER VII.

THE FINAL BLOW.

Martyrdoms of FF. Ortiz and Solinas. Success of F. de Arcé. Martyrdoms of FF. Cavallero, de Arcé, Blende, Sylva, Maco, and thirty neophytes. Antequera usurps the government; persecutes the Jesuits. His repentance and death. Rebels a second time defeated by the Christian Indians. Renewal of charges against the missionaries. Martyrdom of F. Lizardi. Treaty of exchange between Spain and Portugal; forced emigration of the natives. Persecution and deportation of the Jesuits. Present state of Paraguay. Review of the labours of the Society in that country . . 84

PARAGUAY.

CHAPTER I.

SPANIARDS AND INDIANS.

Character of the Spanish colonists. The system of encomienda. First missionary efforts. Arrival of the Jesuit Fathers. Their labours and successes among the Indians.

HOWEVER dark the record of Spanish crime in the settlements of South America, however frightful the cruelties and oppressive the tyranny exercised upon the unhappy natives, no one can read the history of those times with an unprejudiced mind, and still consider the government of the mother-country as being entirely or even greatly responsible for them. From Charles V. of Austria to Philip V. of the Bourbon dynasty, the Spanish monarchs, in fact, invariably took the part of the oppressed against the oppressor; and all their general regulations, as well as all their especial directions to their vice-regal representatives in the colonies, tended alike to the restriction of the power of the conquering Spaniard, and to the amelioration of the condition of the conquered native. That such humane endeavours should have proved a failure might have been a cause for wonder had it occurred in the present day, when facilities for communication have so greatly lessened the difficulty of legislating for a distant people; but that such should have been the case in those times appears the almost inevitable consequence of the distance of the countries to govern and to be governed, the dangers and delay attendant on the communication between them, the total ignorance of the people for whom they were thus called upon to legislate, but, more than all the rest, the vicious character of those to whom the Spanish monarch was perforce compelled to delegate his power.

For it happened then, as it very possibly might have happened even now, that while the good, the just, and the noble-minded remained quietly at home, the idle, the unprincipled, and the desperate, those, in a word, who had lost their fortunes by extravagance, or their characters by excess, sought to repair the one or to redeem the other by a greedy search after gold or a reckless pursuit of adventure in the new world. Men such as these would under any circumstances have thought but lightly of infringing the law; many of them, in fact, had often done so even in their native land. What wonder, then, that with broad seas between them and the legal punishment of their misdeeds, intrenched moreover amid the rocks and fastnesses of the untrodden regions they had made their own, they should have defied with impunity every effort to control their actions; or that the history of the Spanish colonies should in consequence have become one long scene unrolled of rapine, murder, and rebellion; of governors not only defeated in their attempts at restoring order, but deposed, murdered, or sent home blackened by calumny, to die in a dungeon; of bad men gaining the upper hand by means which the good were too scrupulous to employ; and of barbarities exercised on the unhappy natives, beneath which, if they at times revolted, they much oftener pined and drooped and faded away, until the red Indian had well-nigh disappeared from the land which his fathers had possessed in peace, and which for untold centuries they had called their own.

The fatal policy of distributing the Indians *encomienda* among the Spaniards no doubt tended greatly to increase the sufferings of that unhappy race, by giving something of the force of law to an appropriation of native labour which would otherwise have been stigmatised as an act of private injustice. By the regulations of this system, a certain number of Indians were, for a given term of years, parcelled out to individuals, who for two months in every year had a right to their personal service, besides exacting an annual tribute from them; and in return, the master, or "commander," as he was most usually called, was bound to see to the comfort and instruction, both religious and secular, of the natives confided to his care. As originally designed by the crown, these conditions were by no means unmerciful; and had they been carried out by the colonists in a similar spirit, would undoubtedly have led to a much more rapid civilising and Christianising of the Indian population than could otherwise have been accomplished It may, and indeed it must, be objected to the system, that the labour being compulsory, their state was in fact nothing short of slavery. But, on the one hand, we must remember that it was designed for men who, without this restriction as to time, would in all probability have attempted and effected a life-long servitude of the native; and on the other, it is surely an open question whether in reality it may not have been a more humane and equitable mode of dealing with the Indian than that of driving him by main force from his possessions, or cheating his childish simplicity into the exchange of the broad lands that God and nature had bestowed upon him for beads, and gewgaws, and trumpery trinkets,—to say nothing of the deliberate dulling of intellect and shortening of life by the fatal gift of brandy (the fire-water of the savage), in order to blind him more effectually to the ruinous nature of the bargain he was contracting; all which have been the notorious practices of other nations, and more modern and (so to speak, by courtesy) more liberal times.

Whether, however, the means adopted were judicious or the contrary, most certainly the object of the Spanish government was chiefly directed to the temporal and eternal welfare of the people so suddenly and unexpectedly confided to its care; but, unhappily, it never was in a condition to command that rigid adherence to its regulations which was absolutely necessary to insure success. Cruel and rapacious, and divested of all save the externals of religion, the Spaniards thought of nothing higher than the rapid acquisition of wealth by every means within their power. In such hands as theirs the system of assignment rapidly degenerated into a positive slavery; and the natives either died by hundreds beneath the imposition of unaccustomed burdens, or, scandalised by the vices and revolted by the cruelty of their owners, confounded at length the religion which their masters professed with the vices which they practised, and resolutely adhered to that idolatry which had become to them the badge of freedom, while Christianity was identified in their eyes with a state of servitude. In vain Charles V. and his successor Philip endeavoured to regulate and prevent these disorders; in vain an officer was appointed whose especial charge it was to investigate the treatment of the Indians, and to deprive of authority and office all who abused or trespassed on their weakness; the distance of the mother-country proved an insuperable bar to any real or permanent redress, and sixty years had rolled away since the first possession of the land, and nothing effectual had yet been done to advance the cause of civilisation, or to establish the empire of Jesus Christ upon the old idolatries of its heathen occupants.

It was not that the Catholic Church was idle or indifferent; the historian of Peru and Mexico, uncatholic and anticatholic as he is, has yet most truly said, "The effort to Christianise the heathen is an honourable characteristic of the Spanish conquests. The Puritan, with equal religious zeal, did comparatively little for the conversion of the heathen, content, as it would seem, with having secured to himself the inestimable privilege of worshipping God in his own way. Other adventurers who have occupied the new world have often had too little regard for religion themselves to be very solicitous about spreading it among the savages. But the Spanish missionary from first to last has shown a keen interest in the spiritual prospects and welfare of the natives. Under his auspices churches on a magnificent scale have been erected, schools for elementary instruction founded, and every rational means taken to spread the knowledge of religious truth; while he has carried his solitary mission into remote and almost inaccessible regions, or gathered his Indian disciples into communities like the good Las Casas in Cumana, or the Jesuits in California or Paraguay. At all times the courageous ecclesiastic has been ready to lift his voice against the cruelty of the conqueror, and the no less wasting cupidity of the colonists; and when his remonstrances, as was too often the case, have proved unavailing, he has still followed, to bind up the broken heart, to teach the poor Indian resignation under his lot, and to light up his dark intellect with the revelations of a holier and happier existence."

All this, and a great deal more besides, did the Spanish missionaries in behalf of the poor Indians; but how were they to succeed in their appointed mission where every thing tended to neutralise their efforts? How were they to convince the savage of the paramount importance of religion, when he saw among his rulers no anxiety except for gold? How were they to press upon him the necessity of patience, purity, meekness, and humility, when pride, rapacity, cruelty, and revenge, were the chief characteristics displayed for their imitation? Or how were they to tell of the glory of a soul absolved from sin, while the body of the hapless listener was wasting and withering away in chains provided by the professors of the doctrine which they preached? It was, in fact, a hopeless task, so long at least as they could neither promise indemnity to the Christian convert, nor even prevent the very fact of conversion being made a pretext for enforcing the odious slavery of the *encomienda*; and, forced unfortunately by their position to mediate continually between the opposing parties, to preach patience on the one hand, and forbearance on the other, they gradually but surely lost the confidence of both; the Indian dreading them as being of the nation of the oppressor, while the Spaniard hated them as the defenders of the oppressed. Where the Spanish foot had never trod, or the Spanish tongue never had been heard, there the missionary had a fairer chance; crowds would fearlessly gather round him, and won by the beauty of the doctrine he preached, would gladly and eagerly receive baptism at his hand. But the Christian priest was too often, even in his own despite, made the pioneer of the Spanish soldier; as sure as his track was on the mountain, so sure was the searcher of gold to be in his footsteps; and peace and order vanished as he came. The Indian was consigned to the slavery of the mines; his wife and children, yet more unmercifully, sold to the highest bidder in the market; and the unhappy missionary, balked of the fruit of all his labours, was fain to seek out a more distant people, or to remain and break his heart, and wear out his whole existence, in stemming the tide of vice, which gave the poor savage but too plausible an excuse for returning or cleaving to the superstition of his fathers.

It was plain that in a contest such as this no isolated efforts of zeal would avail to victory. A body of men was needed, who would not only scatter seed, but watch its growth; in other words, who would gather the neophytes into congregations, and alike defend them from Spanish tyranny and keep them aloof from Spanish crime. The secular clergy and Franciscan friars were far too few in number fully to carry out a work like this; and at length Francis Victor, the Dominican

Bishop of St. Michael's, finding himself almost without priest or religious whom he could send upon the mission, addressed himself to the Society of Jesus for their aid. They had not, however, waited for this summons to visit South America, having been sent to Lima some time before by the burning zeal of Borgia, the third, and after the saintly founder of the Society, the greatest of its generals. In that city they had built a church and college; and while Father Portilla stirred the masses of the people by his mighty eloquence, Father Lewis Lopez devoted himself to the instruction of the negroes; and the rest went forth among the natives, attended the hospitals, and made themselves all things to all men that they might win all to Christ.

Gladly these apostolic men accepted the invitation of the Bishop to enlarge the theatre of their labours; the success of their missions more than realised his expectations; the Bishop of Tucuman sought them likewise for his diocese; and in 1586 they were received, with almost regal honours, in the city of Santiago. The governor himself, with all his officers, and the chief nobility of the city, came out to meet them; they were conducted through streets adorned with triumphal arches and strewn with flowers; crowds assembled to greet them as they passed; and weeping for joy, the Bishop himself embraced and blessed them, and led them to his cathedral, where a *Te Deum* was intoned in thanksgiving for their arrival. Well might the old man weep for joy; five secular and a few regular clergy being the utmost he had hitherto been able to command for the instruction of the vast and reckless population over which he ruled; while he himself was all but sinking beneath the responsibilities of his position, and his anxious endeavours to fulfil them in his own person. Although the Jesuits felt themselves more especially called to the conversion of the heathen, they saw that all their efforts in that direction would be in vain, if the poor natives were still to be corrupted by the example of those above them in station and intelligence; they therefore commenced their labours by a mission among the Spaniards. It succeeded almost beyond their hopes; for a time at least the latter were won to holier lives; and the Indians, seeing the good effect which had been produced by the preaching of the Fathers upon their rulers, willingly submitted in their turn, and flocked in crowds to hear them. Two of the missionaries had by this time qualified themselves to address them in a language they understood; and after having preached for some days to the Indians of the town, they went forth to those who were scattered through the district, when upwards of seven thousand neophytes, fervent and well-instructed, soon rewarded their zeal. They were placed under the care of a secular priest, and then one of the Jesuits returned to Santiago, while others proceeded by invitation of the Bishop to Cordova, and Father Monroy and a lay brother preached with great success to the nation of the Omaguacas. They were a fierce and indomitable people, who had twice destroyed the town of Jujuy, and proved themselves on many other occasions the dangerous and untiring foes of the young colonies of Spain. But when, after infinite trouble, Father Monroy had succeeded in inducing them to enter into a treaty of peace with the latter, he had the vexation of finding his exertions made worse than useless by the folly of the Spaniards, who enticed two of their caciques into the town, and immediately threw them into prison. They were released at last on the earnest expostulations of Monroy; but he could not prevent the natural distrust which took possession of the Indians, and feeling indeed too certain that it would be impossible to keep them in the practice of the precepts of Christianity, when Christians, alas! were themselves ever ready to corrupt them by example, or to irritate them by cruelty, he led the whole tribe to a spot nearer Tucuman, where he delivered them to the care of a secular priest, while he himself returned to the mission.

The Jesuits were received at Assumption, the chief city of Paraguay, with as much joy and gratitude as had greeted them at Santiago; and there Father Salonio commenced a mission, while Fild and Ortega embarked upon the Paraguay for the country of the Guaranis. These people were not perhaps absolute idolaters, since Charlevoix assures us that they acknowledged but one God; however, their notions on the subject were extremely vague and uncertain, and they neither offered sacrifice nor possessed any established form of worship. They dwelt, for the most part, in the province of Guayra, which is fertile though unhealthy, and abounds in serpents, vipers, and other formidable and disgusting reptiles. The Fathers penetrated into its most hidden depths and wildest fastnesses, and then went back to Assumption to tell their Superior that they had seen two hundred thousand human beings, who, with a little care and trouble, might speedily be gathered into the fold of Christ. They found the plague raging in the capital on their return; but this circumstance only gave fresh impetus to the zeal of the Jesuits, who, not content with their labours for the Spaniards, went fearlessly among the Indians, and had the happiness of bringing hundreds of dying creatures to the knowledge of the true God in the very hour of their entrance upon eternity. Grateful for the charity with which at every risk to themselves the Jesuits had lavished assistance upon them in their utmost need, the Spaniards now showered unasked-for favours upon them, besides building a house and church for the society both at Villa Rica and Assumption. So great was the enthusiasm at the latter place, that the inhabitants of the colony all vied with each other in lending a helping hand; women of the highest rank brought their riches and their jewels, the poor bestowed their labour without payment, and when the Fathers besought them to moderate their zeal, they only answered, that as they were working for Jesus Christ, they could not be afraid of doing too much.

In fact, they had ample cause for gratitude to the Fathers. It was not alone the spiritual assistance which they were ever ready to offer to all alike, whether among the rich or poor, but the Spaniards soon discovered that the Jesuits were their best defence against the resentment of the natives, when their own cruel treatment had lashed them into rebellion. Thus when a troop of Spaniards had suffered themselves, while marching against a party of revolted Indians, to be decoyed into a deep defile where they were completely at the mercy of their foes who were in possession of the heights, Father Barsena, who had been journeying under their escort, came at once and effectually to the rescue. Alone and unaided he sought the encampment of the savages, climbed the rocky ascent from whence they were preparing to rush down upon his countrymen, and spoke to them with so much force and eloquence, that he induced them to suffer the Spaniards to pass without further molestation. This success appears to have given a new direction to his zeal; for separating himself from his countrymen, he remained for some time preaching to these people, who, fierce by nature, and doubly fierce by their habits of intoxication, yet listened to him with respect, and thus received the first germs of religion which with time were to develop into perfection. From their tribe he passed on to the nation of the Lulles, and from thence to the Red River, where being joined by other missionaries, he was recalled in consequence of his great age and infirmities to Cuzco, in Peru. The last of the Incas lay dying in that city —dying, it may be, less of actual disease than of his crown despoiled, his kingdom taken, his people ruined, and his country enslaved. Such a conversion would be a fitting crown and conclusion to an apostleship of life-long labour in the land; so the aged Father thought; and his zeal kindling, he sought out the dethroned and dying monarch, spoke to him of the Christian's God and the Christian's hope of heaven with all the fervour and unction of a saint in his novitiate. heard him, at length, abjure the idolatry of his fathers, poured the waters of baptism on his brow, received his parting breath, and having thus procured him an eternal crown in place of the temporal one of which his own white nation had deprived him, went home himself to die.

A little while previous to these events, Father Romero had been appointed provincial; and after preaching for some time in and about the city of Assumption, and from thence to Cordova and Santa Fé, he advanced, in company of a Spanish gentleman named Jean de Abra, into the country of the Diaguites; a people who adored the sun, offering in its honour feathers which they had previously consecrated, according to their fashion, by dipping them in blood. The Father was received with much cordiality until a certain day, when he was interrupted in his preaching by a band of hostile savages, painted and adorned after the manner they adopt when about to enter on the trial and torture of a captive. In all probability they hoped to inspire terror; but they had mistaken their man. Father Romero merely interrupted his discourse for a moment, to command the new comers to bow down in adoration of the living God, who, as their Creator, had a right to exact such homage from them. His intrepidity probably saved his life; and instead of the attack, which had evidently been meditated, the Indian chief merely declared, in a tone of haughty defiance, that the white men might, if they pleased, degrade themselves in such manner; but that neither he nor his people would stoop to such dishonour, and would still continue to worship according to the traditions of their fathers.

After this protest against the Christian's creed the savages withdrew, leaving Romero and his companion in hourly expectation of a rising, to which they would infallibly have fallen victims; but after a night passed in prayer and preparation, to their great astonishment, the angry chief made his appearance to apologise for his conduct of the evening before, and to promise in his own name and that of his nation greater docility for the future. In fact, that very day upwards of a thousand

Indians accepted Christianity; and all was proceeding well, when the avarice of the colonists once more nearly ruined the mission of the Fathers; for, hearing that the tribe had solicited baptism, and fancying that, because they were willing to embrace Christianity, they were likewise willing to become their slaves, they attempted to distribute some of them *encomienda*; and the Indians, indignant and surprised, at once revolted, declaring that Christianity was a snare and a pretence; and that the Spaniards merely sent their priests before them to reconnoitre, in order that they themselves might ultimately step in and possess themselves of the land. "But it never shall be so!" they cried: "rather thar submit to slavery and the white man's prison, we will fall upon these black-robes and tear them to pieces as traitors and seducers." And so indeed they would have done, had not an old savage, who had attached himself to the Fathers, succeeded at last in calming the tumult; and the first effervescence of popular feeling over, Romero had no difficulty in making them comprehend the disinterestedness of his own intentions towards them, and his freedom from every thing like collusion with the colonists. He concluded by giving them a solemn promise, that the religion which he preached should never be made a pretext for depriving them of liberty—a promise afterwards nobly to be redeemed by the Society to which he belonged; but at what cost to its members and its own reputation, this history will sufficiently make manifest.

CHAPTER II.

SEARCH FOR SOULS.

The Jesuits oppose the enslaving of the natives. Appeal to the king. Manifesto of the Fathers. Rapacity of the colonists. The first "reductions," and the first martyrs. Renewed contentions. Second appeal to the home government, which supports the Jesuits. Expulsion of the Fathers from Assumption.

The favour which the Spaniards had hitherto displayed towards the Jesuits was chiefly owing to the marvellous influence every where exerted by these apostolic men over savages who had hitherto resisted both force and persuasion. It was a favour selfishly bestowed for the sake of the benefit which they hoped it would confer on themselves, and just as selfishly withdrawn the moment they found that the benefit they sought would be absolutely and unconditionally denied them by the Fathers.

Up to the moment of the settlement of the latter at Assumption, the colonists had reckoned with confidence upon their assistance; first for taming the natives, and then for drawing them into the slavery of the *encomienda*. But they little knew the men with whom they had to deal, or the spirit that guided the Christian missionary. Themselves for the most part soldiers of fortune, they could not forgive the boldness which stepped between them and their prey; and blinded by avarice and intoxicated with success, they could as little perceive the wisdom of a course which, if followed out according to the suggestions of the Jesuits, would have given to Spain a new race of subjects, and to her colonies servants instead of slaves—friends instead of enemies, more terrible in their desultory warfare than whole armaments of civilised foes. For although, indeed, the savage could never hope finally to win the day against the might and power of Spain, he yet could, and often did, destroy hundreds in his unforeseen attacks, and his blows unhappily fell full as much upon defenceless women and children as upon the mailed and armed aggressors. It is lamentable to be compelled to acknowledge that a handful of men, for the most part uneducated and of ill repute both in their old country and their new one, as the colonists too often were, should yet, by the peculiarities of their position, have been able to embarrass at least, if not to frustrate, all the designs of a merciful government, and all the efforts of the Catholic clergy, who alone were either willing or able to carry them into execution. Here, however, as elsewhere, the spirit of the Church, which pleaded for the liberty of the Indian, found itself in direct antagonism to the spirit of the world, which advocated his slavery; and here, as elsewhere, the Church has been blamed for what the world has done, and the Jesuits, who acted only on her inspiration, have been accused, in the formation of their Indian congregations, of the pride and avarice of which the world, represented by the Spanish colonists, was actually guilty in opposing their foundation.

Peace, even in outward seeming, could not, of course, be expected long to subsist between parties so diametrically opposed to each other; the one being ever determined to oppress, and the other to oppose oppression. Father Torres gave the first offence at Cordova by refusing to treat the Indians employed in building his church as slaves, and insisting on paying them at the same rate and in the same way as European workmen; and not long afterwards Father Lorençana, in the city of Assumption, was guilty of a yet graver and more unpardonable misdemeanor in the eyes of the Spaniards. The Indians of the neighbouring country had revolted; and the officer sent to suppress the insurrection, instead of searching out the real offenders, fell upon a party of defenceless natives who had taken no share whatever in the rising, and, loading them with chains, drove them like wild beasts into the capital, where they were sold publicly as slaves. It was not in the nature of an honest or true-hearted man to witness such a scene unmoved. From the slave-market, where he had seen the creatures for whom Jesus Christ had shed His blood put up like cattle to auction, Father Lorençana came burning with indignation to the church, and mounting the pulpit (he had already tried the effect of private expostulation in vain), denounced the injustice, and threatened the vengeance of heaven upon the offenders. They heard him without reply; the boldness of the act for a moment silenced all opposition, and even elicited the applause of the people; but when the first enthusiasm had passed away, they began to look upon it with other eyes; and to feel that, so long as the Jesuits were there to oppose them, they would never be able to put in execution their favourite and short-sighted schemes for the acquisition of wealth, by enslaving the Indian nations in the fullest and most unequivocal sense of the word.

Little cared these true sons of Loyola, however, for the persecution which they had thus excited. They might, indeed, and must have felt most keenly the difficulties thrown so recklessly in the way of the conversion of the natives; but for themselves, they had done their duty, and could with confidence leave the result to Providence. The citizens of Cordova rose against them in a body, and driven first from that city, and then from Santiago, they retired to St. Michael's without other regret than such as was necessarily occasioned by the interruption of their mission. At the latter town they were received with kindness, and permitted to found a college and preach to the neighbouring nations; but even there they could not entirely check the rapacity of the Spaniards, and they had too often the misery of seeing the poor Indians carried off, while they were in the very act of preaching to them, to be sold in the slave-market. Such a state of things was not to be quietly endured by really Christian men, and much less by really Christian priests. They appealed to the home government; the King of Spain an swered by a letter which did equal honour to his head and his heart. In it he declared, "that the only yoke he intended for the natives was the yoke of Jesus Christ; for he wished to have subjects and not slaves; to rescue the Indians from the slavery of their own passions, not to subject them to those of other men; and therefore, except in the event of aggression on their parts, he positively forbade any save the missionaries from attempting to reduce them, since they alone could do so in the name of Jesus Christ, and in the spirit of the Christian religion."

Upon the receipt of this letter, both the governor and the Bishop of Paraguay resolved to put every future attempt at the conversion of the Indian tribes entirely into the hands of the Jesuits, who had all along proved themselves such fearless and zealous advocates of the cause of freedom. Joseph Cataldino and Simon Maceta were the Fathers named for this expedition; but, true to the principles adopted by their order, they would not leave the city of Assumption without publicly declaring their determination to oppose henceforth, in the king's name, and at any cost to themselves, every attempt upon the liberty of their converts. "We will make them men and Christians," they said, "but never slaves. They are not a conquered people, and therefore you have not even a conqueror's claim upon them. It is permitted neither to you to deprive them of their freedom, nor to us to be accessory to the fact. The law of God and the law of nations alike forbid it, and therefore we will not do it; but what we can and ought to do, that we promise we will do. We will show them the beauty of peace and order; we will teach them that the abuse of liberty is the worst of slaveries; we will make them comprehend the advantages of living beneath a well-ordered government, and we hope to see the day when these poor savages will learn to bless the hour in which they adopted the religion of Jesus Christ, and became the servants and subjects of a Christian monarch."

Just and noble as were these sentiments, they found no echo in the bosoms of the men to whom they were addressed; and then the Jesuits went yet further. They pressed upon their consideration the slower but much more certain advantages to be derived from the system they wished to pursue. They asked what had become of the thousands of Indians who had disappeared since the discovery of Paraguay; and while they proved that the fearful mortality which had swept them from the face of the earth could be attributed only to the inhuman manner in which they had been overtasked and overburdened, they touched on the improbability of the conquerors being able to keep the land in cultivation, if the conquered were no longer in existence to till the soil.

But it was all in vain. They were speaking to men hardened by avarice, and, by the very pursuit to which they had devoted themselves, narrow-minded and short-sighted even as respected their own interests; and feeling that all their arguments were thrown away, the Fathers at length resolved upon prosecuting their mission elsewhere, and by assembling the Indians in distant villages to guide them to civilised life and to God, far from the interference and bad example of their countrymen. They left Assumption for the purpose; but the report of their undertaking went every where before them, and by the time they reached Villa Rica the ferment was at its height. Not a man in all that city could be found to guide them on their way; and a cacique of the tribe they were going to visit having come into the city for the purpose of doing so, he was thrown into prison, whence he was not liberated until threat as well as remonstrance had been employed. Then, and not until then, the Fathers proceeded on their way. Sailing down the Paranapane (or "river of misfortune," as it is called in the Indian language), they reached at length the spot where the Pirapa discharges itself into its cedar-shadowed waters, and there they **found two hundred Guaranis Christians, fruits of the** former mission of Fathers Ortega and Fild. Advancing a little further up its banks, they came upon upwards of twenty other villages, some already Christianised, and others well disposed to receive the faith. To them the Fathers represented the advantages of dwelling in community, as well for the greater facilities thus acquired for instruction, as for the better protection of their liberty against both colonists and heathen natives; and they had actually agreed upon joining the abovementioned Guaranis, in order to form one settlement with them, when it was discovered that a Spaniard who had followed the Jesuits by way of aiding in their labours had secretly decamped, carrying with him for the slave-trade many women and children belonging to the tribe. It is easy to imagine the indignation of the poor Indians; for they naturally concluded that the Jesuit Fathers were implicated in the transaction, and the latter had much difficulty in vindicating themselves from so injurious a suspicion. Indeed, it is most wonderful how they ever acquired the confidence of the Indians, identified as they were both by blood and language with men who had no god but gold, no law but their own interests, no mercy in war, no truth or even justice when at peace. God alone could vindicate His Church amid such deeds of treachery; and that He did so is most certain; for the poor natives learned at length to discriminate between the Spaniards and their pastors, and, while they loathed and feared the one, to trust entirely and to love the others. The storm which the wickedness of the runaway Spaniard had raised died gradually away, and with an admirable faith in the fair dealing of the Fathers, the Indians allowed themselves to be conducted to the spot where the other Guaranis were already assembled. It was the first of those Christian congregations which, under the name of 'reducciones,' or 'reductions,' gave so many true-hearted children to the Catholic Church, and so many faithful vassals to the crown of Spain; it was called 'Loreto,'—fitting name for an establishment destined to be the nursing-cradle of the faith of Christ in a land where as yet no knee had ever bowed to do homage to His name.

The fame of this young city, and of the wisdom and mercy with which it was governed, soon spread abroad among the tribes; and Indian after Indian flocked into it for protection, until it grew so much too small for its population, that the priests were compelled to found consecutively three additional settlements for the disposal of the surplus. Encouraged by this success, they threw themselves into their work with redoubled energy, straining every nerve to gather the heathen yet more and more entirely into their new foundations. They searched the land from north to south; in the day-time fainting beneath the ardours of a tropical sun, and at night tormented almost to madness by the mosquitoes, and crowds of nameless stinging insects which that warm and humid atmosphere brings forth. Now they wandered singly, or in pairs, over wilds and deserts, where they were liable to become the prey of ferocious cannibals or ravenous wild beasts. Anon amidst forests swarming with poisonous reptile life, and where vegetation grew so rank, that, hatchet in hand, they had to cut their way through the dense and tangled masses which every where obstructed their steps, and veiled the very light of heaven above their heads—in a country too where earthquakes are of every-day occurrence, and hurricanes so terrible, that the mightiest monarch of the forest falls prostrate beneath their fury; where the lightning blinds by a vividness, and the thunder rolls with a continuity of sound, of which we, the children of a more temperate climate, can form but a faint conception; and where, in the rainy season, such floods pour down from the skies, and the rivers rise so suddenly, that travellers in those days were often up to the waist in water, or compelled to take refuge in some lofty tree, or to sleep on the mud which the retiring tide left bare.

More than once the Fathers narrowly escaped with

their lives from these terrible inundations. Upon one occasion, we are told that Father Ortega, after wading for some time up to his middle in water, was compelled, with his companions, to seek safety in a tree. For three nights and days the tide continued rising; and they suffered first from hunger, and then from weakness and exhaustion, while thunder and lightning, and an impetuous wind, which never ceased, added new and appalling terrors to the natural horrors of their position. The wild beasts of the forest, too, came flocking round their place of refuge; serpents of all kinds, rattle-snakes, and vipers, were floating on the waters; and one enormous reptile actually coiled itself round a branch close to the one to which Father Ortega was clinging. For a little while he watched his fearful neighbour, expecting every moment to be devoured; however, the bough most fortunately broke beneath its weight, and it floated away in a different direction. But his own personal perils were not his worst anxiety; for, in the hurry of their first alarm, the Indians who accompanied him had unhappily chosen a tree much too low for safety; and their despairing cries, as from time to time they were forced to retreat from the rising flood higher and higher still among its branches, came faintly to his ears across the raging waters, and pierced his heart with sorrow. So it went on until midnight of the third day; and then one of the Indians, swimming to the foot of the tree, besought him to come to the assistance of his countrymen, most of whom were dying. The Father prepared to do so; but he first bound his poor catechist, who had no longer strength to hold on by himself, to the strongest bough that he could discover; and then throwing himself into the waters, struck out for the tree where his poor companions were expiring. They were almost at their last grasp by the time that he arrived, and only clinging to the branches by a last long effort of desperate exertion: happily he was able to climb into the tree; and in that strange and perilous position, with the wild winds raging round him, and the stormy waters surging at his feet, he received their confession of faith, and baptised them one by one; and one by one, with a single exception, they dropped into the flood, and were seen no more. Having thus done his duty, as none but a Catholic priest can do it, he returned to his catechist; and the waters soon afterwards retiring, they were able to pursue their way. But Ortega bore with him a trophy of that glorious day in a wound, which, as it never healed, became a source of suffering and merit for him to the last day of his life.

Even perils such as these were, after all, far less terrible and revolting to human nature than those which awaited the Fathers who undertook to preach to the cannibal Indians. The four reductions already founded had, by the peace and comfort which reigned among them, become objects of desire to all the other tribes, and one of these applied to the governor for pastors to form them into a congregation. They were notorious cannibals, and even the Bishop hesitated to send among them any of the few missionaries whom he could command, and whom he felt he should thus be devoting to almost certain death, without any adequate success to compensate for their loss. In this dilemma the governor sought out Father Torrez, and told him that he had no longer any hope save in the zeal of his religious. He was answered on the instant. Torrez assembled all the Fathers in the college, and communicated to them in a few words the fears and misgivings of the Bishop; then fixing his eyes on Lorençana, the rector, he added, "My Father, as the Lord once said to Isaias 'whom shall I send, and who will go?'" Instantly, flinging himself at the feet of his provincial, the rector answered in the words of the same prophet, "Here I am; send me." Father Torrez raised and embraced the grey-haired man, already grown old in the labours of the mission; the whole city was in admiration of his courage; and accompanied by a young priest of the society, who was only too happy at being permitted to join him, Father Lorençana set out on his perilous enterprise.

They built themselves a hut and a chapel, the walls of mud, the roofs constructed of leaves and branches; and there they took up their abode in the very midst of the "tolderias," or wigwams, of the cannibals whom they were sent to convert. A year passed slowly on, and save certain schemes for the massacre of the missionaries, which happily were discovered in time to be prevented, nothing of any consequence occurred. Then the conversion of two chiefs created a sensation among the people; a woman, with her daughter, sought baptism; but her husband, against whose express prohibition she had acted, sought out a heathen tribe, and induced them to attack one of the Christian nations, declaring that nothing less than the blood of the last Christian Indian, served in the skull of the last of the Christian priests, could satiate his revenge. Happily his ferocious wish was never to be gratified; the Christians were successful in the struggle that ensued, and numbers of his own tribe becoming converts, Lorençana removed them for safety higher up the country, where a church was built and a new reduction formed under the name and patronage of St. Ignatius.

It was the fifth in order of foundation; and while Lorençana was engaged in its completion, Father Gonzales, after working wonders among the Indians resident on the banks of the Paraná, undertook to ascend the Uruguay from its mouth to its source. This river, of a thousand miles, rises as a tiny rivulet among the Sierra do Mar, the mountain sea-range of the kingdom of Brazil; and under the name of Pellotas, runs for a considerable distance westward, between banks of massive and high-pointed rocks. It afterwards assumes the name of the Uruguay; and as it proceeds, innumerable smaller streams swell its waters, until it becomes a great and mighty river, navigable for large vessels even up to the Salto-grande, or great fall, which lies half-way between the Ybicui and the Rio Negro, the largest and most important of its tributary streams. Upon these lonely waters Gonzales embarked with a few Indian companions to act as guides; and although he did not fully accomplish all that he had undertaken, nevertheless, as it so frequently has happened to others of his brethren, he laid open a vast extent of unknown country to the future investigation of the colonists. The province called Tapé, situated between Brazil and the Uruguay, was the chief scene of his labours. The Indians of this district, who were a branch of the Guaranis and spoke their language, were naturally of a mild and gentle disposition; but dwelling in a mountainous country, they possessed all the love of freedom inherent in mountaineers. This at first made them unwilling to listen to Gonzales; but he had no sooner succeeded in convincing them that their freedom would be safe in his hands, than every repugnance at once vanished, and they flocked in crowds to hear him. Of all the nations of South America, they proved, in fact, the most docile in their reception of the Gospel, and the most faithful in their adherence to it. Their reductions became so numerous on the banks of the Uruguay, that they have given their name to all the other Christian establishments in that province; and thus Father Gonzales, with the loss (as it happened) of no other lives than his own and those of his two companions, first explored this vast extent of country, and then reduced it to the dominion of the Spanish crown.

Recalled by his superiors, he was obliged for a time to leave the new reductions to the care of his two companions; and when he returned in the following year, it was only (in the strictest sense of the word) to give his life for the flock which had been intrusted to his care. The reductions were attacked by a party of pagans; and as neither he nor the other Jesuits who were with him would consent to abandon their spiritual children, they were killed in the *mélée* which ensued. Another Father was soon afterwards sent to supply their place, and he also was stoned to death by the same Indians;

but this time the murder was avenged; for the Christian inhabitants of the other reductions being joined by a troop of Spanish horse, together they attacked and defeated their savage foes, recovered the bodies of the martyred Fathers, brought them in triumph to the city of Assumption, and there interred them with every mark of honour and respect.

It is not surprising that the wonderful facility with which their reductions had hitherto been formed should long ere this have suggested to the Jesuit Fathers the idea of a Christian republic, where, far from the dwellings and evil doings of the colonists, the spirit of the primitive Church might be revived among the fresh young nations of the newly-discovered world. Reason enough they had, too, for wishing to remove the work in which they were engaged out of the reach of European interference, long experience having taught them that it was absolutely impossible ever thoroughly to convert the natives while in the immediate proximity of their Spanish masters; their illegal and tyrannical claims on the services of even the most independent of the tribes, their cruelty to all, their crimes, by which they gave the lie direct to the religion they professed,— any of these singly and alone would have been sufficient reason for making the contemplated separation; but all together they rendered it indispensable to success. Formal application had already been made to Philip III. of Spain; and following the example of his predecessors, who had each cast the weight of his authority on the side of liberty and religion, he answered the remonstrance with a rescript, by which the Jesuits were authorised not only to preserve their converted Indians from the yoke of the *encomienda*, but also to withdraw them entirely into congregations, so as to separate them effectually from all contact with the settlers. The mere rumour of this permission was quite sufficient to rouse the indignation of the Spaniards; but, secure in their good intentions, the Jesuits remained firm, and to every menace and accusation only answered, that with the Indians already in the possession of the colonists they would not interfere; for they were painfully convinced that their labours, at least for the present, would be thrown away on men whom evil example had corrupted and cruelty made desperate; and that their endeavours would be best bestowed on those who had either never yet been in subjection to the Spaniards, or had flung it off altogether. But, reasonable as their answer was, it could not satisfy the suspicions of the avaricious settlers; and to such a height did their discontent arrive, that at last Francis Alfaro was sent as visitor from Spain to arbitrate between the contending parties.

He approached the city of Assumption by water; and as his bark glided through the devious windings of the broad and silvery Paraguay, he was met by a troop of Christian Indians. Their vessel was adorned with green boughs and flowers, and they came perhaps in the hope of winning his sympathy and protection for their people. The young Indian who commanded the party paid his compliments with grave self-possession and respect, and invited the visitor, who was accompanied both by the Governor of Paraguay and by the Provincial of the Jesuits, to finish the journey in his boat. This they accordingly did; and on reaching the shore, they were met by the father of the young Indian chief, who was himself one of the caciques of the nation, and who brought his youngest son, a boy of about two years old, to be baptised by Father Torrez. The Spanish visitor kindly accepted the office of godfather on the occasion, a much easier one than that which had brought him to the city; for the practice of the *encomienda* had worked itself into such a system of absolute slavery, that not even the authority of the king, nor the representations of the bishop, nor the efforts of the governor and magistrates, had hitherto been able to repress it. Nevertheless Alfaro did his duty; and after a long and patient investigation of the circumstances of the case, published a decree by which the enslaving of the Indians was peremptorily forbidden; but the opposition to this decision was of so violent and of so threatening a nature, that, for a time at least, he was obliged to modify it, by permitting the enforced labour of the Indians for the space of one month, on condition of their receiving proper and equitable wages during the rest of the year. Very unwilling was he to make even this concession; and he took care to adhere to the terms of the royal rescript, by excepting from its operations all such Guarani and Guaycuru Indians as had been already converted, or should hereafter be converted by the Jesuits. He also wished to assign to the latter the same salary as was usually given to the secular priests; but Father Torrez, considering it too much for religious, refused to accept of more than a fourth part of the sum. This disinterestedness won him a short-lived popularity among his countrymen; but it passed away as suddenly as it had appeared; and Alfaro had scarcely turned his back upon the city ere its inhabitants rose and expelled the Jesuits, as the authors, or at least the originators, of the decree which had galled them to the quick.

Not long afterwards, however, one of the citizens, touched with remorse, waited on the governor, and in presence of all his slaves, whom he had commanded to accompany him, promised not only to adhere faithfully to the conditions prescribed by the decree, but for the future to treat the Indians rather as his children than as his slaves or servants. So noble a recantation of error naturally produced a reaction in public opinion; the Jesuits were recalled to Santiago and Cordova as well as to Assumption, and, for a time at least, the poor natives received a more Christian treatment at the hands of their Spanish masters. It was, indeed, but a passing gleam of sunshine in the midst of gathering clouds; but, such as it was, the natives felt that they owed it entirely to the firmness with which the Jesuits had advocated their cause; and little wonder was it that those who were already Christians should cling with even greater love and confidence than before to their holy protectors, or that those who yet wandered unreclaimed and unconverted should earnestly invite them to come and settle among them

CHAPTER III.

FIRST FOUNDATIONS.

Paraguay. Character and habits of the natives. The work of conversion and civilisation. Description of a reduction. Its internal government. Occupations of the missionaries. Regulations as to property and commerce.

THE Paraguay, or the "crowned river," which is the signification of the word in some of the Indian dialects, rises in $13\frac{1}{2}°$ south latitude; passing through the rich Brazilian territories of north Grozzo and Cuyaba, it receives the Pilcomaya and the Vermejo on its way, waters the province to which it gives its designation for a distance of six hundred miles, and then loses its name and identity near the city of Corrientes, in the waves of the Paraná.

Very fair and fertile is the land which lies between these sister rivers. The wide savannahs, sheltered by trees and watered by innumerable rivulets, are of as deep and emerald a green as the pasture-lands of England; hills and gently swelling eminences, bright in every variety of tint that forest-tree and flowering shrub can give them, now slope gently down into smiling valleys, or gird anon the still deep lakes that so often come like a beautiful surprise upon the traveller, and shroud them from all save the blue of heaven which lies mirrored in their bosom. The palm-tree, with all its eastern associations of grandeur and of beauty, lifts its stately head upon the sultry plains; there too the orange yields its twofold gift of fruit and flower, and the fig-tree unfolds its dark-green leaf, and offers the thirsty wayfarer its delicious fruit, without price or trouble; while the hills are every where clothed with the noblest and most useful trees that South America can boast. The algarroba, equal in appearance and value to the British oak, and the kapacho, said to be more durable than either; the urand-îg-irac, as beautiful as rosewood; the yerba-tree, the tatayiba, or wild mulberry; the palo de vivora, which in its rind and juice presents an infallible cure for the most deadly serpent's bite; the cebil and curupac, excellent for the purpose of tanning; the aromatic cinnamon; and then, for underwood, the white flowering acacia; the paradise-tree like mountain ash, with its blossom of exceeding fragrance, and its clusters of rich amber berries; the incense-tree, yielding the odour of the pastilla, the palo santo with its sweet-scented gum,—these and a thousand others make thickets of bloom and sweetness under the more lordly forest-trees, and the passion-flower twines its wreaths from bough to bough, and many-coloured parasites deck the highest trees with flower and foliage not their own, and the delicate air-plant, hanging from solitary rock or thunder-riven stump, floats along the breeze and fills it with the odour of its pendent blossoms. Creatures beautiful or dangerous, or both together, stalk through these gorgeous woods; squirrels leap and monkeys chatter among the twisted branches; the puma, vulgarly called the lion, and the ounce, or tiger of South America, crouch in their lonely jungles; and every form of reptile life is there, in its moist marshy places, from the deadly rattlesnake and boa constrictor to the cobra or culebras de bejuco, which looks so like the tree from whence it takes its name, that the unwary traveller, mistaking it for a withered branch, has all but grasped it in his hand ere he discovers his fearful error. But the woods of South America are all astir with animal life; and it would take pages only to name the insects, birds, and reptiles that towards evening fill the air with a murmur of harsh sounds, until it almost seems as if every leaf were a living thing, and had lifted up its voice to swell the discord. Azaro describes no fewer than four hundred new species of the feathered tribe inhabiting Paraguay: the eagle and the vulture haunt its cliffs; swans, black and white, and red flamingoes, bathe themselves in its limpid waters; and every variety of the parrot tribe, from the cockatoo to the paroquet. with fire-flies and bright-winged humming-birds, glance like living gems among the dark foliage of its forests.

It was in the yet untrodden and uncultivated places of this fair land that the Jesuits for the most part settled their reductions; and in the year 1629 they had already succeeded in founding about twenty-one; some in the province of Guayra, or on the banks of the Paraná, and others again on the river Uruguay; when the appearance of a new enemy in Guayra threatened to undo all that had been already done, and to drive back the converted Indian to his coverts, with a yet fiercer hatred for his European oppressors burning in his bosom than had ever been there before.

Instead, however, of proceeding at once to this disastrous era in their history, it will perhaps be interesting to the reader to give a succinct account of the mode in which the Jesuits commenced these foundations, and of the laws and regulations by which they afterwards moulded them into civilised societies. It has been already said, that from first to last the obstacles they had to contend with were innumerable; and if the most insurmountable arose from the bad conduct and rapacity of the Spaniards, there was much also in the habits and character of the Indians themselves to add difficulty to the undertaking. Unused to any authority save the loose rule of an elected chief, whose power could always be eluded by removing from the tribe; accustomed to roam without restraint the woods and fastnesses of their mighty land, its deserts at once their cradle, their dwelling-place, and their grave,—it was equally difficult to convince them of the advantages of a settled mode of life, or to accustom them to the habits of industry entailed by its adoption. Their religion was of the vaguest kind; but for the most part they believed in a supreme Deity and in the after-existence of the soul; a fact sufficiently proved by the care with which they left bows and arrows and provisions in the grave, in order that its occupant might be able to supply his own wants in the world to which he had departed. Their priests were called "maponos," and were usually employed also as physicians; but, as a general rule, they had no external form of worship; and while some among them adored the devils or idols which they called manacicas, and others worshipped the sun and moon, all were superstitious, consulting the songs of birds and the cries of certain animals as auguries to guide their conduct. It has been sometimes said, that the American savage held an indistinct tradition of the redemption, believing in the incarnation of one who should fill the world with miracles, and afterwards ascend into heaven; but how far this idea, if they had it, is to be traced to their intercourse with the Spaniards, it is impossible now to ascertain.

They lived chiefly upon fish, roots, honey, and whatever animals they could snare with the lasso, or shoot with bow and arrows. Hunting was, therefore, one of their chief occupations; while war, as a necessary consequence of their being divided into innumerable small tribes, might be as correctly designated their principal amusement; and the prisoners taken on these occasions being for the most part killed and eaten, they united the natural recklessness of the savage for human life with the fierce thirst for human blood which belongs exclusively to the cannibal. The European, therefore, who went unprotected among them was continually in peril of that fate, the most revolting of any to the mind of man; but not for a moment did this consideration retard the footsteps of the missionary, or shackle the freedom of his actions for the conversion of souls. With his Breviary for his only treasure, and a staff, headed by a cross, for his only weapon, sometimes with a few converted Indians as interpreters and guides, at others with only a lay brother or a second Jesuit to bear him company, he set forth upon his mission. His food was roots and fruits, or a few handfuls of maize, which he carried about his person; his bed the ground, or a slender mat to protect him from the bites of the reptiles, with which those wild places abound; and he had to climb up steep and rocky mountains, to wade through fens and pathless morasses, to pass as best he might over lakes and rapid rivers, or to cut his way through miles of dense primeval forest, before he could reach the savages whom he wished to convert and save. As he drew near their haunts, various and ingenious, and trying alike to mind and body, were the expedients by which he endeavoured to assemble them around him. Sometimes taking advantage of their known love for music, he would go singing through the woods; and when they were drawn to him by the sounds, the pious canticle would be exchanged for an exhortation, in which he set forth his motives for coming among them, and briefly but clearly explained the principal articles of the Christian creed. More frequently, however, the Jesuits drove herds of cattle, sheep, or goats, sometimes across two or three hundred leagues of country; and this plan had a double advantage in it; for it not only enabled them to lure the Indians to them by the prospect of plenty, but also to stock the settlement and to support them in it until they could be persuaded to labour for themselves. "Give us to eat," they would often cry, "and we will stay with you as long as you like." And in order to be able to do so, and thus to convince them of the advantage of living in community, the Jesuits found it necessary both to supply them with food in the first instance, and by hard and downright personal labour to provide for their wants during the course of the next year.

Many of these religious men had been born to wealth and station in the luxurious cities of their native land, or they had been educated in the haunts of science, and had won applause in the chairs of universities; but now, putting aside all love of learning and all thought of comfort, they hesitated not to make themselves seem poor and unlettered, for the sake of Jesus Christ and their love of souls; and so they set to work in earnest, cleared the forest, ploughed the land, sowed barley, maize, beans, pulse, hewed down mighty trees, and brought them for building purposes to the settlement— in one word, became herdsmen, masons, carpenters, labourers, hewers of wood and drawers of water, while the Indian with folded arms looked gravely on, and the Spaniards openly mocked the folly of an undertaking which, because they would not nobly share it, they stupidly chose to pronounce impossible. But time went on, and proved the right. Example was powerful where precept must have failed; and when after harvest-time the savage tasted the fruits of a toil which he had witnessed, but had wisely not been compelled to share, he began really to comprehend something of the advantages which might accrue to himself from a settled scheme of life and labour. From that moment the work of civilisation had commenced; and won first to order and then to God, the Indians soon took their natural places in the colony as its workmen and mechanics, while their venerable teachers were enabled to return once more to their own vocation,—the salvation of souls. The first care both of pastor and of people was the church, which in the beginning was built of wood, but in better times of stone; and though at first they were content to make it simply decent, they were at a later period enabled by the talents of their neophytes to render it magnificent—at least in the eyes of those for whom it was intended. After a time, indeed, the natives became themselves the best artificers; and among the statues and pictures, often royal gifts, which were sent from Europe, the work of the poor Indian held no unhonoured place in the church of his own reduction.

The form of the village which in time grew up around this sacred building was always the same. the church and college of the missionaries forming one side of a large square, and the other three being composed of Indian huts with corridors built in front to protect them from the wind and rain. From every corner of this square, streets, straight and uniform in appearance, diverged in right angles; workshops, storehouses, and granaries, being added as their need was felt. The burying-ground, enclosed by a wall, and planted with palm, cypress, and various kinds of flowering shrubs, was always situated near the church; and a broad walk, marked out by oranges and citrons, with a large cross a. either end, and one in the centre at which funeral processions usually halted for the singing of psalms, led to a chapel, where Mass was said every Monday for the repose of the dead. Thus constituted, the village was surrounded by the chacaras or plantations of the Indian, while in and every where about the settlement were scattered little chapels, for the purposes of processions, connected with the church and with each other by broad avenues of pine-trees, palm, and orange.

When once the mission was thus founded and set a-going, two Jesuits were appointed to minister to its necessities; the one being always in the capacity of a parish-priest, and the other acting merely as his assistant. Each of them was chosen in the first instance by his own superior, who presented three names to the governor, the latter having the power to select between them, subject, however, to the acceptation of the Bishop: but, generally speaking, both these functionaries waived their legal rights in favour of the provincial, who might be supposed best to understand the qualifications of his subjects for the particular missions upon which he was about to send them. Nor was the priest thus chosen absolute even in the fastnesses which he was given to rule; for he was subject to the superior of the missions, whose duty it was to visit them continually, and who in turn was placed under the authority of the provincial.

Both the Jesuit Fathers and their neophytes likewise acknowledged, with the rest of the faithful, the jurisdiction of the Bishop in whose diocese their reduc tion happened to be placed. This prelate visited them occasionally for the purpose of administering Confirmation, and would more frequently have done so had it not been for the expense and difficulty attendant on such journeys; having often to travel for the purpose upwards of six hundred miles through a desert where not a village or dwelling-house was to be seen, where too he had to carry his provisions with him, and to elude the attacks both of cannibals and of wild-beasts. The neophytes, indeed, did all they could to lighten the difficulties of his visitation; they often sent an escort to meet him and guide him through the most unfrequented passes; and besides furnishing him with provisions, they have been even known to lay down roads in order to facilitate his approach. It was high festival-time all during his stay among them; nor were the Jesuit Fathers less rejoiced upon the occasion, it having frequently happened that they themselves requested and almost insisted upon his presence, as the only means of clearing themselves from the unjust suspicions which, as years went on, spread so far and sank so deeply as to be often found even in the highest places of government, whether ecclesiastical or lay. With whatever feelings, however, the Bishop himself may have occasionally entered the reductions, he never left them without sentiments of the highest admiration, and even tears of joy and gratitude to Almighty God, who had made use of the Fathers of the Society of Jesus to change the poor wanderers in woods and devourers of their own kind into practical Christians and good and useful servants of the state. Nothing, in fact, more moderate or judicious could have been devised than the systems by which these results had been brought about, nothing more calculated to promote the true interests of the mother-country by the peaceful and permanent cultivation of the new, and nothing certainly more likely to ensure the true liberty and conversion of the Indian himself, who, but just reclaimed from his native forest, would have been unable to reap the full benefit of the civili sation to which he had been introduced without the slow and certain guidance of a Father's hand.

It has often been asserted, indeed it is almost always presupposed by authors inimical to the Society, that the Jesuits ruled their neophytes without any reference to the imperial power of Spain; yet so far was this from being the case, that the Indians to a man acknowledged the Spanish monarch as their sovereign, and paid a settled tribute like any other subjects. The sum was indeed small, and payable only by those who had reached their twentieth and had not attained their fiftieth year; but the trifling nature of the tribute is not to be ascribed to any want of loyalty on the part of those who paid it, but rather to the clemency of the kings of Spain, who in this and all their other transactions with the reductions invariably showed a generous and truly royal wish to facilitate the conversion of the natives by relieving them as much as possible of the burden of dependence. It was for this intention likewise, and at the especial petition of the Jesuit Fathers, that he constituted the Indians under their charge his own immediate vassals, by which means he freed them from the cruel and ruinous slavery of the *encomienda*, no Spaniard having a right to exact personal service from any one holding land directly under the authority of the crown. Gladly also, when that system had been found a failure, would he have extended the same immunity to the other Indians of the country; but the evil was too widely spread and too deeply rooted to admit of a remedy so simple. It had been tried and had failed already in the hands of more than one visitor despatched by the court of Spain, and experience proved that the Jesuits were right from the very outset; and that it was only where the Indian convert could be kept completely from all contact with the colonist, that he had the slightest chance of escaping the yoke of slavery.

If, however, the king reaped but little material wealth from the actual tribute of the Indians, he found his account in other ways, and by less oppressive means

They always held themselves in readiness to do him service; and whether for public works or for war, the governor was at any time able to levy from them bodies of five or six thousand men, who during the whole period of their engagement were clothed and supported by their own reductions, without costing the government a single piastre.

The civil government of the reductions was carried on by native officials; the cacique, corregidor, and alcaldes being always chosen from the Indians, who were found to submit much more readily to a power which had thus the appearance, at least, of having originated among themselves, although, of course, its acts and decisions were guided and overruled, and especially in the beginning, by the Fathers of the mission. Of these last one always remained in the village for the care and instruction of the resident neophytes; while the other made excursions into the country, to superintend the Indians who were at work upon the plantations, and to instruct such as were hindered by this occupation from being present at the public catechising. Attendance upon the sick was also one of the most unceasing and arduous of the duties of both priests; for newly reclaimed as the Indians were, and unaccustomed to the habits of civilised life, they were not only more than usually predisposed to contract disease, but every disease told with more than usual certainty upon their enfeebled constitutions;—once, in fact, that it took possession of their frames, they seemed to have no power to resist it. Even in healthy or comparatively healthy times, there were always from two to three hundred sick in any reductions which contained eight thousand souls; but if fever or small-pox (the fatal gift of Europe) once set in among them, every home became filled with sick and dying; hundreds were swept away in the course of a few hours, and there have even been not unfrequent instances of the total depopulation of the district. On such occasions every work of spiritual or corporal mercy fell, as a matter of course, into the hands of the priest

Day by day, and one by one, he visited his patients, each being as anxiously cared for and as tenderly consoled as if there were not hundreds of unfortunates around him who were all to be the recipients of the same special and ungrudging kindness. It was, moreover, a necessary duty of the priest to see that the dwellings of the sick were kept with due regard to cleanliness; their food and medicine were prepared at his own house, often even administered with his own hands; in short, he had to watch over the sick, to prepare the dying for their approaching end, and not unfrequently to dig their graves. Compassion for the sick was not a spontaneous virtue among the Indians; they had too great a dread of disease to show much tenderness to the sufferer, and where there was any likelihood of infection, especially where there was even a suspicion of small-pox, they almost invariably fled the spot; mothers deserting their very children rather than run the risk of this loathsome malady. Both upon the civilised Indian, therefore, and his wilder brethren of the woods the fearless self-sacrifice of the Jesuits worked with wonderful effect; and in spite of their terrors, the yet unconverted savages would crowd round and about a pestilence-stricken village, watching the deeds of a charity such as had never been seen in their land before, and which often won them to the faith when prayers, instructions, and exhortations had failed of any effect. The other occupations of the missionaries consisted chiefly in performing the public congregational services, saying Mass, catechising, leading the rosary and night-prayers, giving instructions in the several schools for boys and girls, superintending the adults in the workshops and plantations; all which, with close and frequent attendance in the confessional, not only filled up every hour of the day, but often trenched deeply on those of the night.

Community of goods had been established as a first great principle in the scheme of the reductions, both because it brought these Christian societies into a closer conformity with the primitive Church, and also because it acted as a salutary check upon the natural indolence of the Indian, who, if left to his own resources, would soon have been reduced to beggary; whereas by being made answerable to the commonwealth for the result of his labours, that body took care, for its own sake, that he should contribute his quota to the general store.

However, the Fathers did not allow this rule to be carried so far as to deprive their neophytes of that spur to industry which undoubtedly exists only in the possession of private property. To every Indian, therefore, was assigned a piece of ground for his own especial cultivation; and as he held it rent-free and with the sole condition of his yearly tribute to the king, he was rich just in proportion to the diligence with which he tilled it. At the commencement of the sowing season he received a certain allowance of seed, with the obligation of returning exactly the same quantity after the time of harvest: a pair of oxen was likewise lent him under a similar stipulation of returning them; this precaution being rendered absolutely necessary by the fact, that had the natives considered them as their own they would infallibly have killed and eaten them in any accidental distress that might have occurred. So great, indeed, was their natural dislike of labour, and their propensity to supply their wants by the readiest expedient which presented itself at the moment, that it was found necessary in the beginning to appoint overseers chosen from the most trustworthy and conscientious of the Indians themselves, not only to overlook the labour of the others, but also to see that the cattle lent them were neither injured by over-work and want of care, nor, as has been already said, killed to supply the exigences of a day. As a further precaution against poverty or waste, a large portion of the best and most fruitful land that could be found in the reduction was set aside to be worked, under the direction of steady natives, by the children of the village, who, with so fertile and productive a soil, could easily supply by numbers what they might want in strength.

This plantation the Indians called *tupambaé*, or 'the possession of God,' because its produce was always stored up in the public granaries, from whence it was afterwards distributed by the Jesuits themselves to the sick, the orphan, and new comers, to those who from one cause or another had failed in their own harvest, and to those who by the nature of their trade were incapacitated from attending to tillage themselves. Out of this fund were likewise paid the expenses of those who were necessarily absent, either on the affairs of the colony or by requisition of the king; for, besides the large bodies of men frequently levied for the service of the latter, hundreds of Indians were compelled to reside for months at a time in the Spanish towns, in order to barter their native productions for the merchandise of Spain. Without such an exchange the royal tribute could hardly have been paid, nor could the cultivation of land have proceeded to any very satisfactory extent; for Paraguay contained no mines; and iron. the most essential of all, being imported entirely from Spain, was, after every effort to supply the deficiency, so scarce and so dear as considerably to retard all tillage and to hinder the introduction of many manufactures in which the Indians would otherwise probably have excelled. In exchange for these articles, and others almost as desirable and useful, the natives brought Paraguay-herb,—a leaf employed for the purposes of tea, and to this day, under the name of maté, an article of incessant consumption in South America,—tobacco, honey, fruits, hides, furs, cotton, sarsaparilla, bark, and rhubarb; the medicinal qualities of the two latter, which are indigenous in Paraguay, having been early discovered and made known by the Jesuits. Rafts constructed for the purpose bore these and other productions of their province down their mighty rivers to Buenos Ayres, Santa Fé, and other Spanish towns, where factories had been established by the different reductions. The Indians employed upon this service were absent for months; and out of the sums thus raised they purchased every thing needed by their reduction, having first, as a matter of course, paid the yearly tribute, which was always delivered at the capital of the province and into the hands of an officer appointed for the purpose. Of this tribute, however, the king could in reality be said to receive only a portion; since out of it he not only paid the salaries of such missionaries as he sent to America, but likewise set aside a sum for the purchase of drugs for the reductions, for the wine and oil (both brought from Europe, and expensive) which were needed in the church, as also for a bell, and all the sacred vessels required for the altar, which he invariably presented to each new reduction.

The mercantile arrangements of every settlement were necessarily in the hands of the Indians themselves; therefore, after reading, writing, and the industrial arts, the children were always carefully taught accounts, and instructed in the value of money, besides receiving an insight into the nature and amount of the public revenue.

In the beginning of their missions the Jesuits found the dialects of South America as numerous as its tribes; but they wisely resolved upon employing only one language as a mode of communication throughout their reductions, and having fixed on the Guarani for the purpose, it was taught in all their schools, and has thus become the language of the country, where it is universally spoken to the present day. In addition to this, the children were taught to read and understand Spanish, though not to speak it, the missionaries fearing it would promote that facility of intercourse between the old race and the new which they had found by past experience to be so fatal to the latter. For the same reason also they always chose out wild and unaccustomed places for their intended mission; and in order yet more entirely to enforce the separation of the nations, they obtained a rescript from the Spanish monarch by which all Europeans were forbidden to visit the reductions without an order from the governor or the bishop, or to remain for more than three days. Of course both these functionaries were themselves exempted from the effects of this regulation, which, therefore, could have had no tendency (whatever has been pretended) to leave the Jesuits with absolute authority over the reductions. It simply effected what they intended, which was, to restrict the intercourse of the colonists generally with their converts; but with all their care and caution, they could not always prevent the latter from being maltreated or misled by the former; nor could they entirely obviate the scandal, or the yet worse confusion between vice and virtue, which residence in the Spanish towns sometimes occasioned in the minds of the poor Indians. "How can you tell us," some of them once exclaimed to their missionary on their return from Buenos Ayres, "that modesty or charity are offended by such and such an action, when we have seen white men do it over and over again without compunction?" "Alas, my children," the poor Father could only answer, "I can but tell you that we preach to the white men the selfsame doctrine that we preach to you. It comes from God, and is therefore as unalterable as Himself; and if the Spaniards observe it not, they must give account at the tribunal of the Sovereign Judge, who will severely punish their neglect. Be you, however, faithful thereto, and you will be wiser than the Spaniards, inasmuch as you will secure to yourselves the reward promised to such as, knowing the holy law of God, have the grace and happiness to keep it."

CHAPTER IV.

A DAY IN THE REDUCTIONS.

Church, schools, workshops, &c. Feast of Corpus Christi. Diversions. Religious and moral habits of the people. Their zeal for the conversion of their brethren. Arrival of fresh missionaries. Ravages of the small-pox.

WHEN a stranger, with letters authorising his visit, made his appearance in any of the reductions, he was received in the church by the superior of the mission, the bell was rung, and the children and such as were within practicable distance being assembled, a *Te Deum* was intoned in thanksgiving for his safe arrival—no unmeaning ceremony, where the journey had necessarily been performed amid every danger that wood and wild could present. This done, the traveller was conducted to his lodgings; and if these were assigned to him in the house of the superior, he was waited upon, with equal modesty and attention, by youths who were being educated for the priesthood, and in this, as in all things else in that grave abode, would find the regularity and recollection of monastic life.

The morning after his arrival, a bell would summon him to church; and if he stood for a moment at the gate of the sacred building to watch the people assembling in the great square, he would see the men range themselves on one side, in their poncios and Spanish waistcoats, all of white on working-days, but of various colours on occasions of festivity, and the women on the other, in the long flowing garment called a tipoi, fastened by a girdle round the waist and made of wool or cotton, according to the season, but always of the same snowy hue; while, suspended from a band drawn tightly round the forehead, he would perceive many a little infant quietly reposing on its mother's shoulders; and in all this crowd of men and women he might watch and watch, and still detect nothing, in word, or look, or gesture, inconsistent with the sacredness of the service at which they were about to assist. When Mass was over, perhaps one of the Jesuit Fathers would conduct him to the chacaras, or plantations, where the men were engaged at work, and thence to the schools, in which the girls were being taught to spin and sew, the boys initiated in various trades, and all instructed in reading, writing, and arithmetic; and when he had looked and wondered at these young savages, so patiently submitting to the unwonted discipline of school, and endeavouring to master the tasks which had been set them, then possibly he would be led into the interior of the college, and made familiar with all its mysteries. Usually it was a long low building, overlooking a garden in the rear, and containing, not only the store-rooms and granaries belonging to the reduction, but also the workshops, where the various mechanics were employed at their trades. There, as he wandered from room to room, he would find tailors, weavers, joiners, shoemakers, and carpenters, all cheerfully engaged in their several avocations; and if his visit happened to be paid upon a Monday, he would witness the distribution of cotton among the women and girls, for the purpose of spinning; whereas if, on the contrary, it chanced to be a Saturday, he would see the same cotton brought back spun and ready for the loom of the weaver. Books, too, he would find in plenty; and not merely such as the Fathers might be supposed to have provided for their own use, but such as were suited to the capacity of their neophytes, and which were amply supplied by means of a circulating library established in one of the most central reductions, whence volumes were forwarded to the rest; medicines being distributed in a similar manner by means of a medical establishment in the same reduction.

It is easy to suppose that our stranger would have been tempted also to visit the Indians in their own abodes; and in those huts, built of mud, and roofed with reeds and branches, he would have found it no hard task to make himself acquainted with all the simple arrangements of their daily life; the hammock, carefully folded and put away in the day-time, its owner being then content to sit cross-legged upon the floor; the hollowed stone for pounding maize and manióc, and all the still less artistic contrivances for culinary purposes.

During these and similar investigations, the day would wear almost imperceptibly away; and with the setting of the sun he would hear the sound of a bell once more, and once more see the children trooping to the church for a second catechism, a first having already been given in the morning. The adults would then come in for rosary and night-prayers, and such of the children as had been employed in the tupambaé would be assembled in the great square, to receive a certain allowance, probably an extra one, of provisions, which they were permitted to carry home to their families. Should Saturday and Sunday form any part of the stranger's visit, he would be astonished, perhaps, as well as edified, at seeing these poor savages, who so lately had known nothing of the law of conscience, and who in all they said or did had been guided by their animal propensities alone, now crowding to the confessional with every mark of fervour and contrition; but when, on the following day, he watched them approaching the sacred banquet of the Eucharist, for which many had prepared themselves by days of deep recollection and devotion, and oftentimes by acts of heroic voluntary mortification, the results of which were visible in the very expression of their countenances, he might be tempted to exclaim, in gratitude and delight, "I confess to Thee, O Father, Lord of heaven and earth, because Thou hast hidden these things from the wise and prudent, and hast revealed them to little ones. Yea, Father, for so it hath seemed good in Thy sight."

Did the stranger's visit take place on the eve of

some great festival, he would observe how, by a judicious mingling of amusement with the routine of their daily lives, the Fathers contrived to reconcile their neophytes to a scheme of labour which otherwise would have been all but unendurable to the indolence of their nature. If the feast happened to be that of the titular saint of the reduction, the inhabitants of two or three of the nearest settlements would come with their pastor, corregidors, and caciques at their head, to celebrate it with their friends; the priests also from these reductions would share the labours of the confessional with the pastors of the particular mission, that any who had a difficulty in going to their own superiors might have the opportunity of confession—a wise regulation, which the Jesuits were always careful to carry out yet more entirely, by sending supernumerary clergymen through all their reductions on the occasion of a jubilee, or great indulgence.

If, however, the festival were that of Corpus Christi, each reduction would celebrate it at home, and it would be proclaimed at noon of the preceding day by blast of trumpet and beat of drum; bonfires and rockets, of which the Indians were passionately fond, would illuminate the village in the evening, and bands of children might be seen dancing gaily to the sound of musical instruments, which were made by the neophytes themselves, and on which many of them played with great taste and feeling. In the midst of these anticipatory rejoicings, the preparations for the morning's festival would still be going steadily on, many of the Indians, in fact, having occupied themselves with them for weeks. Some, with their bows and arrows, had killed tigers and other beautiful but formidable animals, whose rich and robe-like skins were needed to lay as carpets of tapestry before the altars; others, with the lasso, had succeeded in securing their prey alive, and with these, carefully chained and guarded, it was the delight of the Indians to grace their processions—much, perhaps, in the spirit in which conquerors of old caused their war-captives to follow their triumphs.

car. Altars, on which the Blessed Sacrament was to repose, triumphal arches, beneath which It was to pass, had been erected at intervals along the broad avenues of the reduction; and both had been adorned with all that nature lavishes of beautiful and sweet in those southern climates. There were garlands of the graceful passion-flower, and boughs of silvery acacia; wreaths of violets and magnificent white lilies mingling with the golden fruit of the orange-tree and the lime. Pineapples every where scattered their delicious odour, and bunches of tamarinds and clusters of ripe bananas displayed their deeper hues among the purple fruitage of the vine, as it trailed its graceful foliage over the trellis-work of the arches. Perhaps a gazelle, bright-eyed and gentle, might be discovered feeding amid all this wealth of beauty; or a young smooth tiger might startle the visitor with its fiery glances; or, from the perch to which they were fastened by a long string, some of the rarest and most beautiful of the feathered tribe might describe airy circles above his head. The eagle, with its eye of light, and its cream-coloured rival, the king of the vultures, would certainly be there; and the pato real, with its rich and varied plumage, and clusters of humming-birds and paroquets, flashing back the sun-rays from their ruffled wings in tints brighter than the brightest jewels the mine can boast; and when the blue night of the south had closed over all, myriads of luminous insects, fire-flies, like wandering stars or sparks of winged fire, would sweep along the summer air, and settling ever and anon, on flower and fruit and thick-wreathed foliage, make them glitter as if powdered with dust of diamonds.

The streets through which the procession was to pass would also be carpeted with flowers and herbs of sweetest odour. The houses on either side, like arch and altar, would be decked with garlands, or hung with tapestry, wrought in that beautiful feather-work then deemed no mean present even for the king of Spain, so rich and various were the colours, and so strange and wonderful the skill with which they were blended together; and each neophyte would be careful also to place before his door baskets containing maize, roots, herbs, grain, every thing, in fine, which was to be sown or planted in the course of the ensuing year, that the Lord Himself might bless them as He passed along. Within the church there would be the smoking of perfumes, and the sprinkling of sweet waters, flowers scattered on the pavement, and lights innumerable burning on the altar. At the conclusion of High Mass a volley of musketry would announce the setting forth of the procession, and the Blessed Sacrament would be borne through the streets beneath a canopy, upheld by the chief Indians of the reduction, while the others followed in regular order, company after company, but all, men, women, and children, lifting up their voices (and the Indians ever sing most sweetly) in hymns of joy and welcome to the living Jesus.

When the religious services of the day had been wound up with Vespers, the Indians would assemble in the great square, where sports of various kinds soon engrossed all their attention. Shooting at a mark, trials of skill with the sling and lasso, were always of the number; but the "sortija," or riding at a ring, was the favourite amusement, as it argued no small share of address and courage in those who were successful. The preparations for this sport were very simple, consisting merely in a sort of door-way made just wide enough for the passage of a man and horse, with a ring suspended by means of a long cord from the upper portion of the frame. At this the horseman rode full speed through the door; and to him who carried off the ring at the point of his wooden dagger was adjudged the prize. It would seem as if the memory of the old festivities in the reductions still lingered among the people; for to this day the Indians of Paraguay delight in acting mysteries such as once were popular among our own countrymen, and continue, in fact, to form one of the chief religious amusements of the German peasants. A stage is erected in the open air; trees, or the branches of trees, are made to constitute the scenery; and here the Indians, both men and women, perform various passages in the life of Christ, and with a simple propriety too (as we are told by an eye-witness) which could hardly have been looked for among actors so untaught. In all probability this amusement was introduced by the Jesuits, in order to familiarise their neophytes with Scripture story; but whether this were the case or not, one thing at least is certain, that at the close of such a festival as has been described, the stranger would have retired without detecting one intoxicated person, or having heard one angry word; and must fain have acknowledged, that after a day of excitement such as might have set all the hot Indian blood boiling in their veins, he had seen those poor neophytes retire in peace and prayer to their homes, leaving no scandal of word or deed to mar the innocent recollections of the day.

Nor is this a fancy picture, or one descriptive merely of some particular period in the history of the reductions. Bishop after Bishop came, visitor after visitor was sent from Assumption or from Spain; and in no one single instance did they leave the scene of their inquiries without bearing ample testimony both to the wisdom and disinterestedness of the rulers, and to the piety and innocence of those who were subject to their government. Great care and diligence of course were needed, and especially in the beginning, to prevent any relapse into habits in which these poor savages had indulged without remorse or check during the greater portion of their lives; and it was, moreover, needful that such vigilance should be exerted in a way sufficiently judicious to prevent its becoming either irksome or irritating to those who were its objects. Innumerable, consequently, but still as wise as they were innumerable, were the precautions adopted by the Jesuits. The Indians generally married at an early age; an arrangement for which the Fathers have been sometimes blamed by those who did not consider the weighty reasons that induced them to authorise this custom. One family alone was allowed under every roof; the sexes were also always kept separate at church, proper persons, called zelators, being appointed to watch over their conduct there; and at night sentinels patrolled the village, who were not only intended to give warning of the approach of enemies or wild-beasts, but whose further and far more important duty it was to arouse the pastor should any scandal or disorder occur during their watch. The regidor, however, was always considered the chief guardian of the morals of the reduction; and if any offence causing public scandal was committed during the week, it was his office to declare it in church on the following Sunday, and to inflict the merited chastisement on the offender.

But these, after all, were merely external restraints, and would, as the Jesuits were well aware, have proved totally insufficient for the end in view, if left without the support of religious principle. It was necessary that they should love virtue and hate vice for the sake of God, and because He has commanded the one and forbidden the other. To effect this great object, they accustomed their neophytes to the practice of frequent confession, and succeeded in inspiring them with such reverence for the Blessed Sacrament, and such an exalted idea of the purity required for communion, that the preparation these poor Indians made was often almost as heroic and sublime as any thing we read of in the lives of the saints. Their spiritual Fathers likewise taught them to sanctify their work by the singing of pious canticles; and by these and other similar means effectually impressed them with so deep a sense of the continual presence of God, and so lively a consciousness of His love for them, that they were ever found quite as unwilling to offend Him in the lonely desert as in the midst of the crowded city. When business, therefore, took them from their homes, neither example nor persuasion could induce them to swear, or drink, or do any thing else which they knew to be displeasing to God; and instances are on record of their reproaching Spaniards with their violations of the Divine law, saying that "nothing good came from Spain excepting wine, and even that by their wickedness they turned into poison." Cruelty and revenge, the normal vices of the savage, were naturally the most difficult to be uprooted; but even here so marvellous was the success of the Jesuits, that, generally speaking (for it is true there were exceptions), hereditary feuds and enmities entirely ceased; the Christian Indian learnt to look upon every neophyte as a brother, whatever the tribe to which he might belong, and as such was ever ready to assist him; so that if the harvest failed in one of the reductions, the rest would vie with each other in making up the deficiency.

Yet this charity, great as it was, was surpassed by that which they exhibited towards their pagan brethren. They would submit to any amount of trouble or ill-usage for the sake of converting even one. If a wild Indian was induced to visit the reduction, they would receive him with every demonstration of joy. The more savage he was, the more prepossessed against them, the more cordially did they welcome him, the more tenderly did they treat him, because they felt that the greater was the hardness of his heart, the greater was the manifestation of love required to win it. They would lodge, clothe, feed him, give him the best of all they had, spend hours in teaching and instructing him; and the day of his conversion, if he was converted, was always one of unaffected rejoicing to the whole reduction. The cannibal Indians were frequently in the habit of selling such of the children of their conquered foes as they did not devour, and these the Christians eagerly purchased; maize, corn, manióc, cloth, all being liberally offered in exchange. If boys, these rescued little ones were confided to the care of the cacique, or chief of the reduction, to be brought up as Christians; if girls, they were given to the most exemplary and well-instructed of the women for a similar purpose; and when they were old enough to support themselves, they each received a house and plot of ground, and were admitted to every other privilege enjoyed by the original inhabitants of the settlement. Another of the favourite duties of the neophytes was to accompany their pastor in his search for souls; and in this they were often of the greatest use, because the wild Indians were far less suspicious of their missionary visitant when he thus came to them in company with some of their own nation.

But if, as it often happened, no Jesuit could be spared to accompany them, they would take this office on themselves; and as soon as the great rains were over, a troop of neophytes, with their cacique at their head, would prepare to leave the reduction, in order to announce the Gospel to their heathen brethren. First, however, they confessed and communicated; then, after obtaining the advice and last blessing of their pastor, they set out upon their pious errand, taking with them a sufficient store of provisions to prevent their being a burden to the objects of their charitable interest.

They went in the spirit and desire of martyrdom, a fate which in fact they often encountered, either through the hardships of the journey or at the hands of their own countrymen; but wherever a friendly tribe received them, there they gave full scope to their loving zeal. With touching earnestness they would explain over and over again the object of the Jesuits in coming among their people, assuring each and all (in order that there might be no misapprehension on the subject) that it was not to enslave the Indian, but to render him happy in this life and eternally happy in the next; and then they would speak of God with such burning eloquence and overflowing fervour, that they often returned to their reduction followed by hundreds of poor heathens, who, thanks to the charity which had thus sought them out in the desert, soon became as devout and well-instructed Christians as those who had brought them to the settlement. Sometimes it happened that the number thus collected was far too great to admit of their being received as permanent dwellers in the reduction; and in this case their instructors would gladly furnish all that was needed for the founding of a new one; not only supplying corn, cattle, and clothing from their own stores, but giving what to an Indian was much more difficult to bestow, their personal and active co-operation in the labour.

The neophytes who, whether from disposition or other circumstances, were unequal to such rough apostleship, gladly made themselves useful in a different way; for example, in teaching their language to the newly-arrived missionaries, resolutely overcoming their natural indolence and dislike to trouble in order to accomplish their task with greater speed and efficiency; and one instance in particular is recorded of a cacique who literally spent his days in translating certain books which he thought would enable the Jesuits to enter more readily and prosperously on their career of Christian conquest.

Burning with such zeal as this for the conversion of their nation, it was only natural they should hail any accession to the number of the missionaries with gratitude and delight. Some of the neophytes were generally sent to conduct the new-comers to their destination; on such occasions they always intoned the *Te Deum* for their safe arrival, and with such an unaffected expression of real feeling, that Father Cajetan Cattaneo, fresh as he was from the exercises of a religious house, tells us he could not behold them sink upon their knees at the verse *Te ergo quæsumus* without being touched to the very heart. This occurred in a court of the Jesuits' College at Buenos Ayres, whither they had been sent to meet him; and severely was their devotion tested, and triumphantly did it stand the test, in the course of the journey homewards. Their route lay up the river, and at first all things went smoothly; safely but slowly, on account of the innumerable sandbanks and rocks that lurk beneath those waters, they coasted along the Plata and the Uruguay, making sail only in the day-time, and at night-fall tying their balsas* to a tree while they landed to cook their supper; never failing, however, first to arrange an oratory of green boughs, where they sung the Litany of our Lady and the *Ave Maris Stella*, and recited the rosary and night-prayers. In the same rustic chapel prayers were said the next morning before starting; and so they went on from day to day, until, on approaching the reduction of St. Michael's, the small-pox broke out suddenly among them. One died; a Spaniard charitably took charge of two others, and conveyed them to his plantation, a little distance up the country; but as it was by no means certain that the infection was stayed, a messenger was despatched to the next reduction with a request for a fresh supply of provisions, in case they should be compelled, as they feared, to encamp in the wilderness. Then they went on with all the speed they could, travelling all day long, and sometimes more than half the night; but the disease had taken steady hold, and it was in vain to endeavour to outstrip it. Four natives were attacked at once; they were immediately parted from the others and put into a separate canoe, and those who managed it made to follow in the rear; but the precaution was of no avail. Again fourteen were stricken;—with such a number of sick it was impossible to proceed. Yet the alternative was sufficiently appalling. A hundred leagues lay still between them and the next reduction, and there was no hope of provisions nearer; for the wild Indians fled in dismay the moment they were aware of the danger. Moreover, only one of the priests understood the Indian language, the other religious being all young missionaries from Spain; and it became a question of grave import whether he should proceed with those who were still well enough to travel, or whether he should stay with such as were to be left behind. If he went forward, the poor sufferers would die unaided; and yet, if

* Vessels formed by lashing two open boats together.

he remained, the others, some of whom doubtless carried the disease about them, would be compelled to meet it without religious assistance. In this dilemma, ten of the Indians voluntarily offered themselves to attend upon their dying brethren. Their services were gladly accepted; Father Ximenes halted with them for a time, administered the Sacraments both to attendants and to patients, prepared the latter for their approaching end, comforted, instructed, and consoled the whole party, and then set off to join the squadron in advance. Happily the brave Indians whom he had left behind, nobly facing death in the cause of charity, were enabled to save half the number of those whose charge they had undertaken. These, when convalescent, they placed on board a couple of canoes; and having buried their dead, crept slowly up the river in order to overtake the main body of the travellers. In the end they succeeded; although no sooner was this great duty accomplished and their charge surrendered, than they fell sick themselves, and all save one perished of the very disease from which they had rescued their brethren; as if God, in His loving approbation of their conduct, could wait no longer, but must needs call them to Himself, in order at once to reward them for a charity which till then was almost unprecedented among their people.

All this time the small-pox had never ceased its ravages even for a day; and thus, burying their dead as they passed along, the strong and the sick went on together until they arrived at a pass of the Uruguay called the "Itu." Here they gave up this vain flight from death. A hundred and seventy were stricken with the disease together; and nothing remained but to land in earnest, to separate the sick from the hale, to build straw-huts for the shelter of the sufferers, and to despatch another messenger in the direction of Yapeju for the purpose of hastening the supplies which were expected from that reduction. They arrived only just in time to prevent starvation, and two months more were spent perforce in the desert, during which the Indians died by dozens, but always in sentiments of fervour and devotion equally surprising and consoling to the Fathers who attended them. At the end of that period the malady abated; and the Father Superior, whom they had at length succeeded in acquainting with their situation, came to their assistance. In a very short time he had arranged and provided all things for their prompt departure; the convalescent he made to travel slowly, in order that their quarantine might be completed before reaching the reduction; but those who had escaped infection were of course glad to proceed as rapidly as they could. The new missionaries were of the latter number; and they had soon the happiness of arriving at Yapeju, where they were received with rejoicing proportioned to the dangers and sorrows amidst which their journey had been accomplished. In that single voyage from Buenos Ayres to the reductions upwards of a hundred Indians had perished; and it may give some notion of their zeal to say, that out of all that number there was not one who did not expire rejoicing in the thought, that he died in the act of introducing fresh missionaries into the country for the conversion and civilisation of his heathen brethren.

The preceding sketch was necessary, in order to afford the reader some insight into the principles on which the reductions were founded, and the regulations by which they were afterwards permanently established. We will now return to their general history, and describe the formidable foe by whom for a long time not only their peace and prosperity were disturbed, but their very existence as a self-governing institution was threatened.

CHAPTER V.

THE MAMELUKES OF ST. PAUL'S.

St Paul's Lawlessness of its inhabitants. Their treachery and cruelty to the Indians. Attack on the reductions. First migrations. Courage and determination of the missionaries. Crimes of the "Mamelukes." The Fathers resolve to evacuate the reductions.

IN one of the provinces of Brazil, and twelve leagues from the seaport town of San Vincente, once stood the city of Piratininga, or St. Paul, the capital of the district to which it gave its name. Built upon a nearly inaccessible rock, hemmed in on one side by mountains almost as precipitous as the height from whence it looked frowning down upon the plains beneath, and on the other by the deep and impenetrable forest of "Pernabacaba," its inhabitants could issue forth at any moment to levy supplies upon the adjoining country, or stand at bay behind the impregnable walls of their rock-built fortress. With such facilities both for offence and defence, it was doubly unfortunate that they should have been the very worst of the worst colonists who had yet visited the new world. At first, between free men and slaves, they barely mustered four hundred inhabitants; but the unchecked license in which they lived soon drew numbers within their walls, which became an asylum for the refuse of all nations—Portuguese, Spaniards, Englishmen, Dutchmen, the last always preponderating,—all, in fine, who had left Europe to escape the punishment due to their crimes, or to follow the lawless desires of their own hearts, flocked to St. Paul's; and when their numbers grew from hundreds into thousands, the citizens flung off the yoke, and even the semblance of the yoke, of lawful authority, and declared themselves independent of the Portuguese crown. Nor had that kingdom the power to dispute the claim; for with their unscalable rock, and their abundant supply of arms and ammunition, as well as the power which they possessed of manufacturing the latter whenever it was needed, they could easily have bidden defiance to a far larger force than any which the nominal monarch of their half-wild territory could have brought to bear against them.

Hence it shortly came to pass that they lived as if they were no longer accountable either to God or to man. They scorned the peaceful arts, as they were scorned of old by the warlike Spartans. Such lands as they possessed were cultivated by slaves, and for the rest they trusted to war and pillage; the slave-trade, in all its naked and appalling reality, being their principal resource. The slave-market of Janeiro was stocked by these marauders. From their city of refuge, where they dwelt on high with the eagles, they would rush down suddenly upon the plains, surround the tolderias, or cluster of wigwams, which constituted the village of the Indians, carry off the able-bodied men for slaves, apportion out the young girls and women among themselves, and put the rest without pity to the sword. Even the other colonists of America were not safe from these attacks; whenever and wherever they could be assailed with impunity, they met with quite as little mercy at their hands as the Indians themselves. The fame of the Paulistas for cruelty and wickedness soon spread far and wide, until, instead of the name which they had taken from their adopted city, they came to be designated as the "Mamelukes," a title significant both to Spaniard and to Portuguese of all the horrors of sacrilege, robbery, and murder, which every where marked the track of these dreaded freebooters.

The Paulistas had thus become the scourge of the land; and all, Spaniards, Portuguese, and Indians alike, had learned to tremble at their name, when the Jesuits appeared in the adjoining province, and by commencing their mission both in Spanish America and in Brazil itself deprived them of the great source of their riches—the unrestricted power of catering for the slave-trade. For wherever the Jesuit came, he brought with him the germs of civilisation and of order. If the wild Indians gathered round him, they were safe, as far as the law of nations could make them so; they were men, and had the rights of men, and could neither be bought nor sold at the will of the European. This the rescript of the Spanish monarch had declared, and this the Jesuits every where enforced in a way that few others in their position would have ventured to adopt. If their neophytes were stolen from them, they followed them to the very camp of the marauder, to beg or buy them from the ruthless enslaver; or they appealed from tribunal to tribunal, from America to Europe, from the viceroy in Peru to the monarch at Madrid, and from the monarch at Madrid to the judgment of the world. They left the extortioner no peace, for they every where published the wrongs of the red man and the injustice of the white; and if every man's hand was at length raised to strike them, if every man's voice uttered evil things against them, if they were finally driven from their reductions upon charges which all the world proclaimed, but which nobody could prove, it is yet impossible to study dispassionately the history of the times in which they lived, and of the men amidst whom they dwelt, and not to feel that, from first to last, the real quarrel of the American settlers with the Jesuit Fathers was, that they set themselves against the illegal slavery of the natives.

The inhabitants of St. Paul were not the men to bear reproach and opposition tamely. In the end they expelled the Jesuits from their city; but at first they seem rather to have resorted to stratagem than to have appealed to the strong argument of war. Probably, with all their recklessness, they had some hesitation at the commencement in carrying bloodshed and havoc into settlements protected alike by the united flags of

Portugal and Spain, and by the sanction of the Church to which, in name at least, many of them belonged. The device which they hit upon was as ingenious as it was cruel; for it enabled them not only to decoy the Indians into their net, but to persuade them that they owed their detention to the machinations of the Jesuit Fathers — the real and only protectors of their freedom. Sometimes they would wander in little groups through the country, planting crosses, making presents to the savages, conversing with them in the Guarani language, which was the most generally understood by both parties; and when they had persuaded them to settle with them in some quiet spot, they led their victims into the vicinity of St. Paul's, when fetters and fire-arms did the rest; or the captain of the Mameluke party, leaving his men crouching among the tall thistles and underwood of the plain, would issue forth alone, clad in the garb of the Jesuits—the "black-robes," as the Indians called them — and drawing them towards him by the magic of the name of Christ, he would speak kindly and gently to them; until a sufficient number having been collected, the preconcerted signal was given, and, his men rushing in, the poor natives were surrounded and carried off fettered for the market before they had even dreamed of a defence. Some of the victims thus ensnared generally made, or perhaps were permitted to make, their escape; and these, returning to their brethren in the reduction, would tell how the false black-robe had spoken peace with his lips when there was war in his heart, and how he had filled their ears with caressing words of love and kindness only that he might lure them with greater certainty to their doom; and with darkening brow and wrathful spirit his savage audience would sit and listen, until they rose in their frenzy to massacre their spiritual fathers; or else,—and it seems almost too sad a tale to tell it,—they fled in sorrow and dismay, to seek, amidst wood and wild and in ceaseless roving, that safety for themselves and for their children which they felt they never could look for among Christian men, since the treacherous blackrobe, in his garb of peace, had proved as cruel as the soldier in his coat of mail.

The suspicion thus created was the greatest difficulty with which the Jesuit had to contend; but he contended perseveringly and successfully. At whatever risk or danger to himself, he left no means unemployed to disabuse the poor Indians of their false impressions. If they sought to kill him, he bowed cheerfully to the stroke; if they were taken captive, he moved heaven and earth to procure their freedom; if they fled from him in hatred and dismay, he pursued them with a love which in the end was sure to overcome all fear, and to restore to him the confidence and veneration of his flock. Alas! it too often happened, that when he had thus, with infinite pain and labour to himself, persuaded his scared children to return, trembling but reassured, to the life of industry which had been so cruelly interrupted, the Mamelukes, emboldened by impunity, came down upon them in undisguised and open warfare, to rob, to burn, to murder, and make captive, sending the Indian once more wailing to the woods, and dashing all the hopes of the missionary to the ground at the very moment when they seemed certain of fulfilment. These dealers in flesh and blood were not long content with the scanty supply of slaves which their stratagems could procure them, they soon brought fire and sword to aid them in their traffic; while the Spaniards, glad at any price to have the storm averted from themselves, shamefully stood aloof, and waited the issue of the unequal contest. So completely, indeed, were they blinded by their prejudices, so entirely, even in those early days, had they learned to regard the Jesuits with suspicion, and to consider the missions a check upon their avarice, —that they could not, or at least they would not see the real value of these settlements, which, interposing directly between them and their foe, might, if properly supported, have been made an almost insuperable barrier to his further advances. The Indians, therefore, were left to defend themselves, and that too without even the ordinary weapons which necessity demanded; for, with its usual narrow-minded misgivings, the colonial government had forbidden the use of fire-arms in the reductions; and it was not until years of expostulation had been wasted, and thousands had perished through the vain delay, that this cruel edict was finally rescinded.

Under such circumstances, the young colonies in Brazil were easily destroyed; and the reductions of Guayra were the next to be attacked. In the universal consternation which prevailed, at first no defence was attempted or even thought of, and reduction after reduction went down before the invader. At length, laden with captives, the Mamelukes appeared before Incarnation; but at the first note of danger, Montoyo, who was then provincial, rushed to the spot, arrested the flying Indians, exhorted them to turn and rescue their captive brethren; and while hastily arming them for the fight, despatched Mendoza, the Jesuit Father of the reduction, to try and negotiate with the foe. A shower of arrows and a volley of musketry greeted his approach to the hostile camp. The Father was wounded, and a neophyte killed at his side; but still undaunted, he sought out the robber-chieftain, told him to his face, and in the midst of his Mamelukes, that he was outlawed alike of God and man, and then, assembling the Indian captives, he cut their bonds, and actually carried them off in the face of the whole army; the very boldness of the act, and perhaps some lingering respect for the character of the priesthood, preventing the troops from attempting to oppose him. An interview between the provincial himself and the Mameluke captain followed, and the latter was ultimately induced to withdraw his troops; but it was only for a time. In the course of that very year the governor of Paraguay passed through the reductions at a moment when nine hundred Mamelukes and two thousand wild Indians, their allies, were known to be assembled at St. Paul's, and only waiting his departure to rush down upon the missions. Yet the provincial, who had dared so much already, in vain implored him to send troops to their assistance With fair words, and unmeaning congratulations upon the vast amount of good which he acknowledged had been effected, he passed on from the threatened province to the city of Assumption; and the Jesuits were left to defend their neophytes if they could, or to perish with them if they failed.

The day of strife was hastened by an accident. A poor prisoner had contrived to escape from St. Paul's; and having sought protection at St. Anthony's, Father Mola, the pastor of that mission, refused to give him up. In revenge the Mamelukes fell upon his congregation, killed numbers at the very foot of the altar, to which they had fled for refuge, and carried off hundreds into captivity. A few of the wretched inhabitants succeeded in escaping to Incarnation; others, sullen and despairing, withdrew into the woods; and there, seized with the old maddening suspicion of the treachery of the Jesuits, they rushed out to seek Father Mola, with the intention of putting him to death. They found him sitting among the ruins of the reduction, and plunged in the deepest grief; yet he had to argue long and seriously with these unhappy creatures before he could convince them of the injustice of their suspicions. When this was once effected, they became amenable to reason; and prevailing upon them to abandon their desolated home, he led them first to St. Michael's, and afterwards further still to the colony of the Incarnation. Father Mansilla, of the former reduction, followed him soon after with such of his neophytes as he could persuade to move. Many, however, refused to accompany him, he returned therefore as soon as he had left the fugitives in safety; and as the Mamelukes were then approaching, he at length induced them to retire and seek safety in the woods. Hardly had they made their escape, when their village was sacked and burned by the foe; yet, painful to relate, the indignation of the poor bewildered creatures fell on the very man to whom they owed their deliverance, and Father Mansilla narrowly escaped their vengeance with his life. The accusation which had been brought against Father Mola was renewed in regard to this good religious; the Mamelukes, to further their own nefarious designs, took care to propagate it in every direction; and as these were all young colonies, and neither sufficiently grounded in the faith nor sufficiently convinced of the real motives of the Fathers to be invulnerable to suspicion, it had its full effect upon the inhabitants of St. Michael's. With some difficulty Mansilla succeeded in removing their misgivings, and the Mamelukes passed on from the destruction of their reduction to that of Jesu-Maria. From the latter place they carried off a crowd of captives. The Fathers resolved upon a rescue; but the enemy being far too numerous to be attacked by any body of Indians they could at the moment have raised against them, they determined, instead of fighting, to follow the Mamelukes into Brazil, and to remonstrate with the captain-general of that province respecting their conduct.

The fugitives were soon overtaken; but at the sight of his poor neophytes drooping alike with sorrow and fatigue, one of the Fathers could contain himself no longer, and rushing, in spite of the muskets that were pointed at him, and the insults and blows that were showered upon him, into the midst of the captives, he embraced them one by one, loudly demanding in pathetic accents either that they should be restored to freedom, or that he should himself be permitted to share their chains. Some of the Mamelukes reviled, some threatened, many scoffed at him as a madman; and one alone in all that number was moved by pity to give up to him such of the captives as had fallen to his share, under promise, of course, of a future ransom. This success did but encourage the Father to greater efforts; and seeing the cacique Guiayvara among the prisoners, he put the chain that bound him round his own neck, declaring he would not take it thence until he had obtained his freedom. The Mamelukes grew angry, and in the discussion that ensued he was more than once on the point of having his brains blown out; but his determination and his utter indifference to danger won the day, and the cacique and a certain number of the other Indians were at last surrendered. Guiayvara was astonished, as well he might be; he had long been wavering between his idol-worship and the Christian creed, and during all that period of irresolution had behaved with the utmost barbarity to this very Father. But now, as he felt the chains fall from his limbs, he threw himself in a very passion of gratitude at his benefactor's feet; and when he was afterwards sent home under the security of an escort, he could only satisfy his deep consciousness of the debt he owed him by going from reduction to reduction, every where proclaiming the charity of the Father, and exonerating his brethren of the Society from all suspicion of collusion with their foes.

In the meantime the Mamelukes, finding their captives disappearing through the intervention of this good Father, resolved to rid themselves of his presence, and decamped one day without him. He fell back upon Father Mansilla, who had been left a little in the rear; and after a short consultation, they resolved still to follow in the distance. There was no room for hesitation about a path, the route lay clear before them, marked out by the dead and dying; and on they went, their footsteps every where arrested by the sick, the helpless, and the weak, whom the Mamelukes had dragged as far as they could, and when they could drag them no further, had left to perish in those dismal wilds. The Fathers did all that was in their power for each unhappy group: they baptised the catechumens, confessed the neophytes, consoled all with the hope of a future life; but they could not remain with any, for their mission called them onward still. On to those who, perchance at no great distance, lay dying the same miserable death; on to those who, yet more unhappy, should live to reach the city of the captives, where chains and cruelty would destroy the body, and despair or bad example too probably kill the soul; on even further still from St. Paul's itself to the slave-market of St. Paul's – the city of Janeiro—there to lay before the governor the outrages and wrongs that had been heaped upon their people. They reached it at length, exhausted by fatigue and sorrow: yet even there they might not linger; for the governor was at All Saints', and to him the authorities of the port referred them. He may have had the wish—it is not very clear that he had the power—to aid them; though he received them kindly, and appointed a commissary to repair with them to St. Paul's to assist in obtaining the liberation of the Indians. A commissary, without troops to enforce his orders, was little better than a mockery at St. Paul's. The inhabitants refused him admittance; the Jesuits who accompanied him were cast into prison: nor was it without earnest expostulation on the part of their provincial that their deliverance was effected; yet when at last they returned to their reduction, it was only to find their neophytes — those for whose sake and for the sake of whose kindred they had endured all this toil and grief — possessed with the same injurious suspicions against them as had before prevailed in the other reductions; and it required all the eloquence of their past labours, and all the indignant remonstrances of Guiayvara, to restore to them the confidence of their flock.

It would be but a sad and weary repetition, to tell of all the reductions that one after another fell a prey to the Mameluke invaders. The wretched inhabitants were driven from place to place; and except to negotiate their liberation, or to rescue them by force from the foe, their pastors never left them; following still to heal the wounded heart, and to bind up the broken reed, and to keep alive the light of faith, which, amid cruelties such as these, might well be supposed to burn dimmer in their bosoms. In one other instance the poor victims rose against their spiritual father; but he succeeded in escaping into the woods, where some of his brethren had taken refuge with the remnant of their neophytes. He found both pastors and people overwhelmed with affliction; and in all that multitude there was not one who had not to mourn the loss of a wife or husband, sister, son, or daughter—either carried off in chains, or murdered in cold blood before their eyes. Nevertheless, they built themselves huts, and sowed what grain they could collect; for they thought that at least in that vast solitude they might hope to remain at peace; but the corn had scarcely sprouted, when the Mamelukes were once more upon their track, and once more they were compelled to fly. These disasters, and many others as bad or worse, at length convinced the Fathers that the work of civilisation which they had undertaken was simply impracticable so long as they remained in the vicinity of St. Paul's. Their neophytes might, indeed, and often did, defend themselves effectually for a time; but it was not possible that a professedly rural population should be ultimately successful against men who were for ever in the saddle, whose only occupation was fighting, and who gained their livelihood by the spoils of war. Sometimes the Mamelukes marched upon the reductions in open guise of battle; at others they broke suddenly out of ambush, or obtained admittance under false colours and on feigned pretences. Not a day or an hour in which they might not be concealed within a few minutes' march of the mission. They came down like a whirlwind on the labourers in the sowing or the harvest time; or they surprised them in the festive meeting, or burst upon them in the hour of prayer. No Indian could feel certain that he should reap what he had sown, or inhabit the house which he had built; nor could he reckon, either for himself or for his wife or children, upon one hour of freedom beyond the one which he was actually enjoying; and, lest the picture that has been drawn be considered an exaggeration, it may be as well to add, that in the official account of the state of the province, called especially *De Missiones*, it is expressly declared by Commissioner Albear, that in one year (1630) no fewer than sixty thousand Indians, and those for the most part torn from the reductions, were publicly sold in the slave-market of Janeiro.

It was plain, that with such an enemy in the vicinity and perpetually on the alert, the Indians never could remain in peace; and after much mature consideration, the Jesuit Fathers finally resolved to transplant their people to a safer distance. One or two of the younger reductions were first removed: the inhabitants were recent converts, and much opposed to the measure, some even absolutely refused to stir; but they paid dearly for their obstinacy, by subsequently falling into the hands of the Mamelukes. In fact, it became more and more apparent from day to day that the whole line of missions as originally laid down must be entirely and irrevocably abandoned. An army of Mamelukes was pressing on to Villa Rica; another swarm of these banditti had appeared on the southern coast of Brazil, threatening ruin to the Spanish settlements in that quarter, as soon as it had overleaped the barrier of the missions; and after one more futile effort to obtain assistance from the commandant of Villa Rica, who, indeed, by this time had quite enough to do on his own account in keeping the enemy in check, the provincial finally resolved upon evacuating the reductions of Our Lady of Loreto and St. Ignatius, which, having been hitherto unmolested, had been the chief refuge of the Indians from the ruined missions.

Both these colonies were situate on the Pirapa; and as they were the last to be abandoned, so they had been the first to be established in the province of Guayra. Both, therefore, by this time vied with the Spanish towns in the size and beauty of their public buildings and the order and cultivation of the sur-

...ounding chacaras; while in both the inhabitants had become thoroughly Christianised, most of them having been born in the bosom of the Church, and all well grounded both in faith and practice. Of their fidelity to their religion they were now to give a signal proof; for, in truth, it was no light sacrifice they were called upon to make. To leave the settlements when they were only just beginning to taste the fruits of their industry; to begin again that life of toil and privation which had already cost them so dear, to go forth once more into the wilderness, and cultivate anew its arid wastes, and that too with only a bare possibility of reaching their destination alive, and a certain prospect of danger and misery to be encountered in the attempt,--all this would have been a trial to the faith of any people; but to the Indians, so indolent by nature, so deficient in foresight, and so prone to look no further than the exigencies of the hour, the struggle must have been terrible indeed. Yet, when Father Cataldino assembled them in the grand square and announced the resolution to which his superiors had arrived, instead of murmuring and resisting, as the Indians of the younger settlements had done, they with one accord consented to the measure, as the only means that remained for preserving their faith and freedom. "To you, our black-robe Fathers," so they replied by their most ancient chieftain, "to you we are indebted for our knowledge of the worship of the Almighty Father, and all the blessings that knowledge has bestowed upon us You have made us Christians,—to you we look that we may so continue; and therefore, wherever you our Fathers, go, we, your children, most willingly will follow. What if hunger, and thirst, and weariness befal us? you will give us of the Bread of Life, and our hunger will be assuaged; and in the strength of that Sacrament our toils will be forgotten. And if our loved ones fail us, if our aged fathers and mothers, our young wives and tender babes, sink beneath the sorrows of the journey, we shall know that they have but gone to the grea Father a little sooner than He would otherwise have called them; and we will not weep for them in their graves,—we will rather follow them in our thoughts to heaven, and rejoice with them in their gladness."

Such, without exaggeration, was the noble spirit in which these poor Indians met the proposition to abandon their smiling homes; and then, with a holy insensibility, which the resistance offered by their countrymen under similar circumstances proved to be not the effect of constitutional indifference, but an act of supernatural virtue, they returned for the last time to their dwellings, stripped them of all that could tempt the rapacity of the enemy, packed up the ornaments and sacred vessels of the altar, and followed the Jesuit Fathers, first to the banks of the Paraná, and afterwards, as they had promised, wherever they chose to lead them.

CHAPTER VI.

THE RETREAT ON THE PARANA.

Disasters and sufferings of the emigrants. Spaniards continue to molest the old reductions. Flight of the inhabitants. Renewed attacks of the Mamelukes. The Indians, allowed the use of fire-arms, defeat the marauders. New settlements. Intrepidity of the missionaries. Bernardin de Cardenas, Bishop of Assumption. His charges against the Jesuits. The fable of the gold-mines. Insurrection of the colonists quelled by the Christian natives.

THREATENED as they were on the one hand by the Mamelukes, on the other by the wild Indians, as cruel and as fierce; menaced even by the jealous avarice of the Spaniards, who could not see without alarm, as it bore on both their present and future interests, the fatal depopulation of the country which such wholesale emigration must produce,—the retreat of so large a band of fugitives was certainly a measure beyond all sober calculation of success, and as such may by many have been stigmatised at the time as rash and ill-advised. It was, however, inevitable; and, moreover, it was planned with a foresight, and conducted with an energy, a courage, and a perseverance, that, had its projectors been warriors or statesmen instead of simple ministers of the Gospel, would have won them honourable mention in the history of the world.

Beautiful from its source to its conclusion,—beautiful, but full of dangers, is the river to which they were about to trust their fortunes. Forests,—the glorious forests of America,—clothe a great portion of its banks, presenting to the dazzled eye every tint of colour, from the sober green of the primeval forest to the bright blue and scarlet, snowy white, and imperial purple of the brilliant parasites that climb the trees and overtop them; the cayman lurks by the sedgy shores, and tigers are even found amid the endless wild-flowers and shining evergreens of the thousand clustering islands that fling grace and beauty over its waste of waters. Often, too, after the rainy season, when the river rises and becomes as tumultuous as a storm-rocked ocean, fragments of these islets are detached from the parent soil; and being kept together in a solid mass by the thick interlacing of the rooted shrubs, go wandering down the tide like gigantic baskets of flowers and foliage committed to its keeping; nay, it has sometimes happened that a tiger has been made an unwilling traveller on the "camelote," as these floating gardens are called; and tradition even records how one of these fierce tenants of the woods, after a journey of uncounted leagues, arrived safely at Monte Video, where he gravely stepped on shore to the unspeakable astonishment of the terrified beholders. Upon the banks of this fair river, but much nearer to its source than to its junction with the Paraguay, the Jesuits with their neophytes encamped; and here they remained for weeks incessantly employed in building balsas by means of strong bamboos. Seven thousand at last were finished, no smaller number being sufficient for their transport; and in these they embarked their neophytes, men, women, and children, only just in time to escape the vengeance of the Mamelukes, who were already on their track. Fair winds and sunny skies cheered them in their enterprise until they reached the Salto-grande, or great cataract of the Paraná, where the river rolls impetuously over eighteen leagues of rocky barricade, roaring all the while like thunder, dashing its spray to the very clouds, and sweeping all before it as it leaps madly down into the dark and boiling abyss below. Here they were compelled to disembark; and three hundred empty balsas were launched upon the rapids, in hopes that some among them, clearing the fall uninjured, might enable them to proceed without further delay upon their voyage.

For one breathless moment of suspense the light skiffs seemed to play and tumble on the seething waters; then they were suddenly lifted over; and when the spectators looked again, they beheld them dashed into a thousand pieces, and floating in fragments far away on the stream below. All hope of continuing their voyage being thus destroyed, the remaining boats were perforce abandoned; and every man took his staff and bundle, every woman her most helpless child; and so, with stout yet saddened hearts, they set off for the foot of the cataract, where all their toil and trouble were to commence again.

For eight whole days they wandered thus, feeding on roots and berries, and such wild game as their arrows could bring down, and drinking of the chance torrent by the way, or of dew deep garnered in the cool cup-like leaves that grow beneath the shadows of the forest. No accessible path lay parallel to the river; nothing therefore remained for them but to plunge boldly inland, their route taking them sometimes over sands burning beneath the rays of the southern sun, sometimes along precipices where one false step would have dashed them to their doom; but oftener still through dense and tangled forests, where trees, the growth of a thousand years, were laced and interlaced with creepers which, thick and strong as the cables of a man-of-war, yielded no passage excepting to the hatchet, and when at last, and after the loss of numbers who died by the way of famine and fatigue, the poor wanderers reached their destination, it was only, as has been said, to begin again the work of preparation on which so much time and toil had already been expended. With weakened forces and diminished hopes they had again to encamp for weeks, while they cut down trees, and fashioned them to their purpose, burying hundreds all the time whom starvation and overwork had hurried to the grave. In defiance, however, of difficulties and disasters, the required number of balsas was in the end completed; and then the Fathers arranged the march by dividing the

Indians into three large bodies, of which the first was to penetrate yet further inland, the second to coast along the river, and the third to float slowly down its waters. To these last the easiest lot might seem to have been apportioned; yet it was not so in fact, as the river-passage included many dangers from which the others would be exempted. The great fall, indeed, had been passed; but, besides sunken rocks and cross currents occasioned by the islands, there were frequent rapids, smaller than the first, yet perilous withal, and many a boat was sunk, and many a life was lost, ere they succeeded in reaching their destination. Patience and perseverance, however, had their reward; and the Jesuits had at last the satisfaction of seeing their scattered neophytes assembled on the banks of the Jubaburrus, a little stream flowing westwards into the Paraná.

They had been watched with jealous eyes, plotted against, thwarted as much as it was in the power of their enemies to thwart them,—all, indeed, but attacked upon the road; and if something of honourable pride were mingled with the first consciousness of success in the bosom of Montoya, the projector and chief director of the expedition, it was soon overpowered by a feeling of sadness when he came to muster the survivors, and found that, out of the vast multitudes who had peopled the old missions of the Guayra, there were but some few poor thousands left to answer to the call. Happily they had been guided by Providence to a fair and fertile territory; although, with all their endeavours, they had much privation to endure until the coming of the harvest,—the Jesuits meanwhile doing what they could towards supplying the wants of their neophytes by devoting to the purchase of corn and cattle the salaries they received as missionaries of Guayra. And now it was that the Spaniards might have learned at last, had they been capable of receiving the lesson, the real value of those reductions which they had so ungenerously refused to defend; for no sooner was this barrier removed than their own immediate possessions were overrun by the Mamelukes, conjointly with hosts of pagan Indians, who were only too happy to avenge their own wrongs by helping the Christians to destroy one another. Province after province was laid desolate, city after city became the scene of their depredations, and both Cividad and Villa Rica were sacked and destroyed, notwithstanding the heroic efforts of the Bishop of Assumption, who went out himself to intercede in their behalf; and nevertheless, untaught by all that had come and gone, the Spaniards, incredible as it may seem, still continued to harass the reductions which remained, by laying claim, on all sorts of unjust pretences, to the personal services of the inhabitants. Once, twice, they asserted these pretensions, the third time they drove the Jesuits from their missions, and replaced them with secular priests; who, although actuated by the same good-will towards the Indian converts, did not possess the same power for their protection as the Fathers of the Society, whose authority was derived direct from the throne itself.

The experiment had well-nigh proved fatal to the reductions. Terrified at the prospect of the slavery which they felt too surely to be in preparation for them, the inhabitants every where fled into the desert; and when at a little later period the royal audience of La Plata commanded the restoration of the Jesuits, it cost the Fathers far more time and trouble to lure back the frightened and indignant savages to their homes than it had taken to assemble them in the beginning. Previous, however, to this decision, the Jesuits had appealed both to Rome and to Madrid against the assaults of the Mamelukes and the iniquities of the slave-trade, Father Tano having been sent to the one court, and Montoya to the other. Both returned with favourable answers, the rescript from Spain containing an especial clause, by which all Indians converted by the Jesuits, whether of the province of Tapé or of the Paraná and Uruguay, were declared immediate vassals of the crown, and as such invested with the same immunity from personal service as was already enjoyed by the Guarani Indians. The amount of tribute to be paid by the reductions was settled at the same time; although, in consequence of the poverty resulting from recent disasters, it was not actually levied until the year 1649, just nine years after it had been regulated by law. The publication of this edict caused immense commotion, and the more so because, over and above the especial privileges conferred upon Indians converted by the Jesuits, it absolutely forbade and declared unlawful all buying and selling of natives for the future. The merchants raved against the Jesuits as the authors of this blow to the slave-trade; while, on their part, the Fathers declared to a man that they would do their duty, and resolutely enforce the law by every means in their power. So furious was the excitement, that their college at Janeiro narrowly escaped being sacked; they were violently expelled from that of St. Paul's; Montoya found it necessary to retire for a time to Buenos Ayres; and the vicar-general nearly lost his life in the tumult which followed his promulgation of the law.

In the midst of all these commotions the Mamelukes had not been idle; and, encouraged by their successful destruction of the Spanish towns, they pushed on to such of the reductions as had hitherto escaped their fury. At that of St. Theresa, after having despatched their prisoners to Brazil, and done all the mischief in their power, they had the audacity to request the Jesuit Father of the ruined mission to say Mass for them in the church. It was not an opportunity to be neglected; he accordingly consented; and the instant the Divine Sacrifice was concluded, he ascended the pulpit, and there upbraided them in the strongest terms for their unchristian conduct. The barbarians listened to him unmoved; they were too far gone in wickedness to be either excited to anger or softened to repentance by a recapitulation of their crimes; and the only symptom they gave of a better feeling, was the presenting the Father who had so earnestly addressed them with the

Indian acolyths who had served him at the altar. The reductions on the Uruguay were the next to suffer; although, being numerous and long-established, they made a vigorous defence. But the struggle was too unequal. The neophytes would not make use of poisoned arrows, nor could they lessen the number of the foe by killing such captives as they could not prevent escaping—a practice constantly and unscrupulously resorted to by the Mamelukes. Fire-arms likewise, as it has been already observed, the Indians were not permitted to possess; and thus, forbidden to wage war in a Christian manner, and unwilling to do so after the fashion of savages, they were necessarily placed at a serious disadvantage. Retreat became the only alternative; and this time the Jesuits secured the safety of their colonies by locating them in that part of the province (entre Rios) which, being surrounded by the Parana on the one side and by the Uruguay on the other, possesses a natural barrier against all invasion. About the same time also Father Montoya, after innumerable negotiations, succeeded in obtaining an edict from Philip IV. permitting the use of fire-arms in the reductions; and from that period a feeling of confidence both in the government and in themselves seems to have grown up among the Indians, and given them new vigour in their own defence; we consequently hear less and less of the Mamelukes as our history proceeds. The neophytes fought bravely, and repeatedly repulsed them; and in one of the last great battles in which they measured their strength with these inveterate enemies of their race, succeeded in so thoroughly routing them, that the death of Father Alfaro, who had been shot in cold blood before the action by a Mameluke soldier, was terribly avenged.

Having thus given good proof of their valour, and exhibited a discipline and steadiness in war in which the Spanish mercenary was often deficient, the Indians were continually called upon to serve in the king's army; and in more than one rebellion of the province the governor owed its suppression in a great measure to their strength and numbers. All this, however, was the work of time; and while the consolidation and defence of the reductions already established gave full occupation to not a few of the Jesuit Fathers, others were as actively employed in the formation of new settlements. Father Antonio Palermo, in company with a party of fervent neophytes, had already coasted along the Paraná, and returned with a multitude of converted Indians, whom he speedily placed in a new reduction; others sought out the poor Indians who had fled to the woods and deserts from the fury of the Mamelukes, and were in danger of relapsing into their primitive barbarism; while others, again, at the earnest request of the Bishop of Tucuman, endeavoured to carry the Gospel into the wilds of Chaco. The nature of this country rendered it particularly difficult of access, its vast and trackless plains, which in summer were one arid waste, being in winter flooded like a sea. The savages themselves were cannibals, and, as a matter of course, the first party of Jesuits who ventured among them were put to death, one of their companions having first been devoured before their eyes; but the two who followed had better success. These were the Fathers Pastor and Cerqueira, and they resolved first to seek out the Abipones, who dwelt on the eastern extremity of the desert; but falling in with a tribe of the Mataranes by the way, they succeeded by kind and gentle perseverance in winning their confidence. Nor did the Abipones themselves prove less accessible to kindness, although they were among the fiercest and most intractable of the American savages, being absolutely in a state of primeval wildness when Father Pastor thus succeeded in penetrating into their haunts. No sooner did they perceive him coming from afar, than they hastened to meet him; and with skins spotted and painted according to their notions of a warrior, eyes darting wild and ferocious glances, hair long, matted and dishevelled, and clubs and javelins, which they whirled with savage outcries round his head, they rushed in upon the Father, and surrounded him and his companions on all sides. Had he shown any sign of alarm, he would probably have been murdered on the instant; as it was, he explained to them his errand, at the same time declaring his confidence in God and in their good faith as simply and as quietly as if they had been but a band of children whom he had interrupted in their play. The effect was magical. Fear would have provoked violence, defiance would have insured it; but such calm and intrepid courage astonished and overawed them, as a thing which they had never witnessed before, and which surpassed their comprehension; and throwing down their weapons, they welcomed their visitor with a shout of joy. From that moment he was their guide, their councillor, and their chosen friend. He instructed them in the rudiments of civilisation; he taught them to abhor their savage banqueting on human flesh; he studied the bent of their minds and dispositions, and succeeded at last in at least partially reconciling them to the settled life of the converted Indians.

So far every thing had proceeded prosperously; when, unfortunately, the numbers of the Jesuits, at all times too small for the work in which they were engaged, were still further diminished by an order from the Council of the Indies forbidding any save Spanish subjects to preach in the colonies of Spain. This restriction was caused entirely by the intrigues of those who sought by all ways and means to hinder the formation of new reductions, seeing that they invariably became so many harbours of refuge from the iniquities of the slave-trade. It was subsequently rescinded; but in the mean time it operated with fatal effect alike upon the colonists by whom it had been prescribed, and upon the Indians, who were the immediate sufferers; for the result was so greatly to reduce the Jesuits in number, that, in order to supply the wants of the old reductions, it was found necessary to withdraw Father Pastor from those whom after so much risk and trouble he was just beginning to civilise. They parted from him with tears, and for days and months looked anxiously for his return; but indignant at last at the long delay, they became the worst enemies the Spanish colonists had yet encountered, and taught them by sad experience all the inestimable advantages that might have resulted from the establishment of permanent reductions in their deserts. They had not yet, however, given this terrible lesson to the Spaniards, when the enemies of the Jesuits received an important addition to their ranks in the person of Bernardin de Cardenas, the new Bishop of Assumption, who threw all the weight and influence of his position into the scale in favour of the slave-trade. He was a man of brilliant talents, but irrepressible ambition; possessed of every quality calculated to gain popularity with the multitude, and never scrupling to prostitute his highest gifts to win their adulation. An informality in his consecration had rendered it in the opinion of many null and void; and the question of its validity having been referred by himself to one of the colleges of the Jesuits, they were conscientiously compelled to declare against it. From that moment he never ceased attempting by open violence or secret intrigue to drive them from the city. The governor, a weak but conscientious man, in vain endeavoured to oppose him; nature had especially gifted him for the office of a demagogue, and he became the idol of the colonists. He addressed himself at once to the one darling interest of their narrow hearts, and worked up afresh all the old leaven of jealousy that lay fermenting in their bosoms by denouncing the Jesuits as the Quixotic apostles of Indian liberty. It was precisely their best title to the love and admiration of all good men; but it was also, and Don Bernardin knew it well, that which excited the fear and hatred of every slave-holder in the land. One hint was sufficient for such an audience; and when he had succeeded in thoroughly rousing the passions of the multitude, he suddenly assumed an air of inspired authority, declared aloud his hypocritical regrets for the step he was compelled to take, and then and there excommunicated the whole body of the Jesuits, forbidding the faithful to hold further intercourse with them. The governor attempted to interfere; but the citizens to a man sided with their Bishop. He had promised them the slave-service of the Indians as soon as the Jesuits should be driven from their reductions; he had hinted, moreover, at gold-mines, which, according to him, lay hidden in their missions; and the idea was far too tempting to these worshippers of mammon to be easily relinquished. They rose as by one accord in defence of the man who had called up these golden visions before their eyes; and it was by force alone that Don Gregorio succeeded in the end in expelling him from the city which he had demoralised by his ambition and scandalised by his crimes.

But the serpent had left his sting behind him. He had whispered of gold-mines; and gold-mines of course the colonists ever afterwards clamorously affirmed to be actually existing among the mountains where the Jesuits had fixed their abodes. Henceforth no story was too ridiculous for promulgation, or too extravagant for belief; and no witness, however despicable his character, but was regarded as trustworthy, so long as he gave his testimony in favour of this imaginary El-dorado. One man actually deposed on oath that he had met an Indian bearing three large sacks of gold upon his shoulders, being a present from the provincial of the Society to the colleges of Cordova and Assumption. The governor treated this base perjurer with the contempt which he deserved, dismissing him with a satirical assurance that he was greatly edified by the disinterestedness of the provincial, who out of so large a treasure had reserved nothing for himself; and at the same time gently hinting his suspicions, that had his informer been similarly circumstanced, he would hardly have practised as much self-denial. Notwithstanding this summary dismissal of the subject on the part of the governor, the report had spread too far and sunk too deep to be thus easily disposed of. It had reached the ears of the Council of the Indies, and had even found an echo in the bosoms of the chief ministers of Spain itself; it was therefore necessary, if only for the sake of the accused, that it should be sifted to the bottom. So the Society thought and felt; and they offered accordingly to evacuate the reductions with all their Indians, in order to leave them more thoroughly open to the investigation of their foes. This proposition was not accepted in the letter, but an officer was appointed to visit the reductions in which the gold-mines were supposed to be concealed; and although the man who pretended to have seen them, and who was to be brought to the spot as a witness, contrived to make his escape on the way, the visitor still proceeded, and never left the scene of his scrutiny until he and his assistants had searched both hill and valley in vain for gold. A second and a third commission to the same place, to other places, to every place, in fact, pointed out by the maintainers of the golden theory, were at different times appointed, but always with the same result; and after years thus spent in useless investigations and harassing suspicions, some of the most vehement accusers of the Jesuits, unwilling to die, as they had lived, in the propagation of a lie, deposed upon their death-beds to the utter falsity of the accusation, and the sordid motives for which it had been invented. The innocence of the Jesuits was thus clearly established; but the consequences of the accusation were not so easily to be undone. Calumny against any body of men almost invariably proves an undying thing; and such it now became to them. A slur had been cast upon their labours in behalf of the poor Indians—a slur most perseveringly maintained by those who best knew its falsehood; the love of riches and the love of power had been put forward as their motives for deeds which the love of God could alone have prompted, and His power alone have made successful; and from that moment they were watched by the Council of the Indies, and by an ever-increasing party in the court of Spain, with a jealousy which never rested until it had expelled them from their missions.

The immediate result, however, of the inquiries was to reinstate the Jesuits in the good opinion both of the home government and of the local authorities, and peace was restored between them and their traducers; but it was only for the moment. By a most ill-timed courtesy, Don Bernardin was permitted to return from exile; and the governor dying suddenly, the Bishop, with his usual promptitude, seized upon the government, and drove the Jesuits from the city. Against this violence they protested, by naming Father Nolasco, Superior of the Order of Mercy, as their judge-conservator, to examine into the charges preferred against them; and his sentence in their favour having been confirmed by that of the royal audience of Charcas, and by the decision likewise of the commissary-general, whom the King of Spain had deputed to judge between them, they were restored by royal command to their college, and Don Bernardin deposed from his bishopric by the Pope, who bestowed it in 1666 on Don Gabriel de Guillestoqui. Even six years before this restoration to their rights, the Fathers of the Society had had an opportunity, and had not refused it, of doing signal service to their enemies. The Indians in and about the city of Assumption had risen in a body against their Spanish masters, and after massacring the principal inhabitants in cold blood, had taken possession of the town. There was no time, had there been the means, for the raising of troops, and the governor was forced to fly; but his situation was no sooner made known in the reductions than a body of neophytes were sent to aid him; with their assistance the insurrection was quelled, the Spaniards delivered from their peril, and the governor enabled to return in peace to his ruined city. The conduct of the Indians on this occasion was, or at any rate ought to have been, an unanswerable argument in favour of the system which the Jesuits had so earnestly advocated. The Indians of the *encomiendas* were in open and successful insurrection when the Indians of the reductions fought in favour of peace and order side by side with men who, far as the poles asunder from them in country, habits, and education, yet possessed an overwhelming claim upon their sympathy and co-operation in the Christian creed which they professed in common.

But although the enslaved Indians had been thus subdued, those who were yet unreclaimed from paganism continued to harass the Spaniards in all directions. Force of arms and peaceful treaty were equally unavailing. If they were defeated on the eve, it was only to do battle again on the morrow; and if they made peace when compelled by reverses to simulate friendship, it was but to break it the moment that the chances of war were in their favour. The false policy of the colonists now reacted fatally upon themselves; for as the Indian had found neither faith nor honest dealing among them, so he would give them neither faith nor honest dealing in return. In this dilemma, the governor turned for assistance to the Jesuits; two of them instantly undertook a mission of peace, and throwing themselves into the midst of the savages, pledged their word for the present sincerity of their countrymen. It was enough: the Jesuits, at least, had been always true to their professions, and the Indians could not refuse to believe them now. A truce for six years was offered and accepted, and this time the savages kept their word; for they had pledged it to men who never had, and, well they knew, who never would deceive them. The Spaniards profited by this long interval of repose to repair their late disasters; and the Jesuits also put it to use in another fashion, by penetrating deeper into the woods and wilds of Paraguay than they ever had done before, and thus giving wider extension to their schemes for the conversion and civilisation of the natives.

CHAPTER VII

THE FINAL BLOW.

Martyrdom of Fathers Ortiz and Solinas. Success of Father de Arcé. Martyrdoms of Fathers Cavaliero, de Arcé, Blende, Sylva, Maco, and thirty neophytes. Antequera usurps the government; persecutes the Jesuits. His repentance and death. Rebels a second time defeated by the Christian Indians. Renewal of charges against the missionaries. Martyrdom of Father Lizardi. Treaty of exchange between Spain and Portugal; forced emigration of the natives. Persecution and deportation of the Jesuits. Present state of Paraguay. Review of the labours of the Society in that country.

It will be remembered, that after Father Pastor's first successful attempt with the fierce savages of Chaco, he had been compelled, by an unfortunate diminution in the number of the missionaries, to withdraw from his new reductions; and that the Indians, thus deserted, had become the most deadly enemies with which the Spanish colonists had yet been called upon to contend. For nearly twenty years the province of Tucuman was continually devastated by their incursions; and although the Jesuits had tried again and again, they had never succeeded, during all that period, in recovering the confidence so unhappily forfeited. However, in the year 1683, with which the present chapter opens, two of the Fathers, Ruiz and Solinas, with a zealous ecclesiastic of the name of Ortiz de Zarate, set forth from Jujuy for the purpose of once more resuming the interrupted mission. In sixteen days they reached the "Santa," called *par excellence* "the Mountain of Chaco," which on clear days commands an unbroken prospect of the country towards which they were directing their steps; yet when they attained the summit, although the sun was high above their heads vast dense clouds of mist, roll ing beneath their feet, shut out the landscape entirely from their view. It was a fitting omen for the commencement of a mission which was to open heaven to those who undertook it, but to leave the people for whose sake it was undertaken still wrapt in the clouds of idolatry and error. They succeeded, indeed, in building a chapel, and inducing some of the Indians to settle peaceably around it; but one morning, at the dawn of day, when they were about to offer the divine sacrifice, a body of savages rushed from the woods with fearful shouts and cries of triumph, killed Fathers Ortiz and Solinas by repeated blows of their *macanas*, or clubs, and then, cutting off their heads, carried them away to make drinking-cups of the skulls. Father Ruiz happened fortunately to be absent, having been sent to Tucuman for provisions; but as he was known to be returning, a party was sent out to intercept him. By a special protection of Providence it missed him; and when he arrived at the reduction, ignorant of all that had occurred during his absence, he found it lonely and deserted; the inhabitants driven by terror into the woods, and the mutilated bodies of the martyrs lying cold and bloody on the altar-steps.

The news of this catastrophe only fired the Jesuits with fresh enthusiasm; and a college was soon erected at Tarija, on the borders of the province of Charcas, to serve as a dépôt of missionaries destined for the desert. Father de Arcé was appointed to lead them on; and twice he tried, and twice he failed, after having been each time cheered on at the outset by some delusive prospect of success. The enterprise was then abandoned for the time, and he turned his steps towards the nations of the Chiquitos, or Little Indians; a name derived, not from the shortness of their stature, but from the extremely diminutive appearance of their dwellings. Divided into innumerable small tribes, this people inhabited a vast extent of country, which watered by the rivers Guapay and Pirapiti, is broken by mountains and overshadowed with forests. They were brave, active, and energetic; and having up to the period of Father de Arcé's visit been in a state of perpetual hostility with the Spaniards, had formed the subjects of a lucrative traffic to the inhabitants of Santa Cruz, where a regular company had been organised for buying up all prisoners made in war for the purposes of the slave-trade. The advent of the Jesuits with their rescript in favour of converted Indians would, of course, put a stop to this illegal traffic; and the Santa Cruzians therefore did all they could to impede the mission. Their real motive they did not, for shame's sake, venture to avow; but they hung about the Father, and overwhelmed him with civilities, magnifying all the while the dangers he was likely to encounter, the blind hatred of the Indians, the frightful insalubrity of the climate, and the contagious diseases which even at that moment were raging among them. To all this, and much more besides, the Father listened with grave politeness; but when it was his turn to answer, the only notice he took of their alarming representations was to exhort them earnestly to lessen the evils of which they spoke, by aiding him in his mission; and when they refused, he left them, to proceed upon his journey. They had not certainly exaggerated the danger, for the plague was raging in the very first village which he entered; but it proved a happy circumstance in the end; for while it could not damp his zeal, the services it enabled him to render to all without exception won him the confidence of the survivors. A church was built, and a reduction founded; and another tribe having expressed a wish to see him, he sent them word to come at once, that he might receive and bless them as his children. The invitation was instantly accepted; and the reduction thus formed having been removed to a more healthy situation on the river St. Michael, another was without delay established on that of Jacopo.

During Father de Arcé's absence at the latter place, the Mamelukes attacked St. Michael's, imagining that, from its being so recent a foundation, it would prove an easy acquisition. But the Chiquitos were naturally a far more warlike people than their old victims of the Guarani nation; and they prepared gallantly for their defence. Father de Arcé, however, being absent from the reduction, they were unwilling to begin the combat without the assurance of his blessing. He returned just in time, heard the confession of every fighting-man, gave them Communion on the battle-field, and before the sun had fairly risen they had attacked and entirely defeated the foe. Their success gave an absolute and unexpected development to the young mission of the Chiquitos; new settlements were as rapidly and so idly founded; and the republic thus suddenly created soon vied with that of the Guarani Indians. The Jesuits pushed these advantages far beyond the nation with which they had commenced; and tribes which the Spaniards had never known or had known only by the devastations they committed—among others, the Lulles, one of the fiercest and hitherto most intractable of all —were in a very short time converted and civilised.

The Father Cavallero—and his life is but a sample of what hundreds of other missionaries were doing at the same time—spent his days in passing from nation to nation, every where announcing the Gospel, every where, as a necessary consequence, braving the death which finally overtook him; but every where subduing the savages among whom he had cast his lot by the power of his doctrine and the sweetness of his words. Sometimes he was openly menaced with their vengeance; at others he only narrowly escaped the snares laid cunningly for his life; but still, unmindful of fatigue or danger, he proceeded boldly and perseveringly on his way. Innumerable reductions marked the spots where his steps had been, and his journeyings were one long triumph of the cross, until he reached the country of the Puizocas, which was destined to prove his grave. An arrow from a hostile savage pierced him between the shoulders; he still had strength to plant the **cross** he carried in the ground, and there he knelt in **prayer** until he finally expired beneath the repeated blows of the macanas. It was the 10th of September 1711. His martyrdom was the signal for many others. The Fathers de Arcé, Blende, Sylva, and Maco, with thirty of their neophytes, perished beneath the clubs of the Payaguas in a fruitless attempt to navigate the Paraguay; while Brother Romero, with twelve other Indians, were murdered by the Zamucos in a sudden fit of rage. Hardly had they done the deed, when they fled to hide themselves in the mountains; and there, believing themselves safe alike from the vengeance of Heaven and the reproaches of the Jesuits, they were still boasting of their recovered freedom, when Fathers de Aguilar and Castanarez, who had followed to appease their anger, entered their tolderias. Such untiring charity was not to be resisted, and the savages followed them quietly back to their old reduction of St. Raphael, where they commenced again the life of labour and instruction which this murderous outbreak had so lamentably interrupted.

Neither these nor any other of the massacres which from time to time occurred had power to interrupt, hardly even to retard, the plan of operations which the Jesuit Fathers had traced out for themselves. Where one man fell, another was always ready to step into his place; and while new reductions were continually being formed, the old ones were just as constantly advancing towards the moral and material prosperity contemplated by their founders,—a prosperity not materially affected even by that rebellon of Antequera which at one time had nearly threatened to dissever Paraguay from the Spanish dominions. Strictly speaking, Antequera was not the governor of the province, having been sent by the royal audience of Charcas merely to settle some disputes which had arisen between the actual governor and his subjects; but the charge was too tempting for his ambition, and instead of mediating between the contending parties, he seized the government for himself, and maintained it by force of arms. The province being already in a factious state was easily induced to declare in his favour; and as the Indians of the reductions were the only part of the population that took no part in the revolt, the Jesuits by whom they were directed became the objects of his suspicion. They were expelled in consequence from their college at Assumption, notwithstanding the earnest remonstrances of Don Joseph Paloz, the newly-appointed coadjutor-bishop of the city, who showed himself an angel of peace and mercy through all the stormy events that darkened his episcopate. On his part, Antequera endeavoured to justify his illegal violence towards the Fathers by first raking up all the old exploded accusations against them, and then inventing new ones. The story of the gold-mines was, of course, revived and made the most of, as best calculated to find favour with the multitude; and their passions were yet further excited by a promise of the plunder of the reductions whenever they should be subdued, and an assignment of the inhabitants to the colonists as slaves. But the usurper had pledged himself to more than he could perform. Ere half his plans had been accomplished, the Council of the Indies put forth all its strength, and the Jesuits were restored by an edict to Assumption; while Antequera was brought back prisoner to Lima, under sentence of death for his rebellion. At that awful hour, with the fear of death before him, the veil fell from his eyes; he confessed the injustice of which he had been guilty, and gave signal testimony of his sincerity by begging to be attended in prison by some of the very men whom he had so cruelly persecuted. At once responding to his appeal, several of the Fathers hastened to share his confinement; and Antequera, selecting one to prepare him for his doom, besought him not to leave him even for a moment; moreover, he declared to all who saw him the utter falsity of the accusations he had brought against them, and prepared a paper to the same effect to be read before the execution of his sentence. Yet all this failed to reinstate them in the good opinion of the Paraguayans; so much more easy is it to sow falsehood broadcast than afterwards to uproot it; and their very attendance on him in prison, and afterwards on the scaffold, though in both instances in compliance with his own earnest request, was construed into an insolent triumph over a fallen foe. Antequera had been a favourite with the people, and his death, far from tranquillising them, roused the yet smouldering embers of discontent. The city of Assumption revolted outright; a junta was named for its government; riots and excesses of every description followed, during which the Jesuits were once more expelled; and despairing of effecting any good among a people thus self-abandoned to their passions, the Bishop refused to lend to their proceedings the sanction of his presence, and left the city. Zavalo, a nobleman of high standing and repute, was sent to quell the insurrection; but finding the citizens in favour of the junta, he fell back upon the reductions, where seven thousand Indians mustered at his call; and thus supported, he marched against the town. War, with all its miseries, ensued; but after months of varying fortune on either side, the rebels were finally defeated; the heathen Indians, who at the first note of war had armed against their Spanish masters, were overpowered; and peace and order being thus restored to the province, the Christian Indians marched back to their reductions, there to face a far more fearful foe than any they had left behind them, in the famine which the absence of so many of the working-members during the sowing-season had necessarily occasioned.

The very fact of this rebellion having been repressed entirely by the Indians of the reductions told with fatal effect upon the popularity of the Jesuits. Men who in their frantic hatred had already driven them from their homes by raising a senseless outcry, without show of justice or pretence at a trial, were not likely to love them better now that by means of these despised natives, whose liberty they had preserved and whose characters they had formed. their own seditious plots and covetous designs had been so shamefully defeated. But, disarmed and powerless, baffled and disappointed as they were, the colonists of those days were not the men to let a victim go unscathed merely because it had for once escaped them. Open violence had failed; intrigue and calumny were left them, and these they plied without pity or remorse. With characteristic audacity they changed at once from rebels into loyal subjects; and affecting an intense anxiety for the interests of the very crown against which they had so lately been in arms, they poured in memorial after memorial, first to the Council of the Indies, and then more directly to the court of Spain, denouncing the authority exercised by the Jesuits in their reductions as derogatory to that of the Spanish monarch, and accusing them moreover of embezzling enormous sums due to the government from the converted Indians. The Fathers met these accusations in the only way in which it was possible to meet them, that is to say, by an earnest petition for a legal trial; and in the year 1732 a commission was in consequence issued, empowering John Vasquez de Aguero to proceed to America for the purpose of investigating the latter and more tangible portion of the charge. The result of this inquiry, concluded just four years after it had been first instituted, proved that, owing to the variety of epidemical diseases which continually desolated the reductions, there was an inevitable variation from year to year in the numbers of the population; but that the tribute had always been paid exactly according to the numerical lists sent in by the Jesuits, and that, these lists being on examination found to have rather exceeded than understated the actual proportion of inhabitants to each reduction, the Society was clearly acquitted of any design of defrauding the revenue. Don Vasquez added, that so far from the reductions possessing the enormous wealth which was supposed to exist among them, the tribute, if augmented, as the colonists were clamorous it should be, would be come so insupportable a burden to the Indians, that it would probably end by their throwing it off altogether. This decision, the result of testimony taken on the spot and after repeated conferences with the governor, the bishop, and other officials of the province, would have satisfied the king, even if he had previously entertained any doubts, which certainly he had not; and he readily followed the advice of Don Vasquez with reference to the tribute, which up to the period of the expulsion of the Jesuits remained at precisely the same ratio at which it had been fixed in the beginning.

Meanwhile neither the vexations attendant on this dispute, nor the previous more open persecution, had caused the Fathers to relax in their efforts for the conversion of the heathen. The desert of Chaco was once more attempted, and this time at the especial request of the viceroy, who found it absolutely impossible to reduce the inhabitants without their aid. Lizardi, Chomé, and Pons obeyed the call; but when they found that an army was to march into the country with them, they positively refused to accompany it. It was not by the sword that they had hitherto won the Indians to obedience; and neither by the sword, nor in company with the sword, would they now undertake the enterprise. Alone, therefore, and with no other weapons than the Cross and the Breviary, they set out upon a mission which had already brought death to so many of the Fathers. A reduction was soon formed by their united exertions within seven leagues of Tarija, and it promised to become a most flourishing settlement. But some rumours of the intended army had probably already reached the more distant portion of the desert; for the Chiriguanes of the Cordilleras, the tribe they were especially in quest of, every where fled before them. In vain they explored mountains, forded rivers, searched the depths of almost impenetrable forests, not a savage could they see or hear of; and they had come in considerable perplexity to a halt, when word was brought them that the tribe they were seeking were assembling in great numbers and in hostile guise near the reduction of the Conception Hither Lizardi flew at once for the protection of his neophytes; but finding all things apparently calm and tranquil on his arrival, he supposed he had been misinformed, and prepared to offer the Adorable Sacrifice. Scarcely, however, had he reached the altar-steps, when, from the woods and mountain-fastnesses where they had lain concealed, the Chiriguanes came pouring into the village, put the terrified neophytes to flight, and carried the missionary off in triumph. Amid blows and insults they dragged him on, until, half-dead already with the treatment he had received, they set him on a rock as a target for their arrows; and when a day or two afterwards the neophytes ventured to return to their deserted village, they found the Father on the spot where his foes had left him, his body pierced with arrows—his Crucifix at his side, and his Breviary open at the office for the dying, as if he had sought to recite it over himself during the long and lingering agony that must have ushered in his death. Pons, who had accompanied him in his expedition to the desert, returned to take charge of the bereaved reduction, while Chomé was sent forward in search of souls. To make amends for this disaster, the fierce tribes of the Zamucos were formed into a reduction by the Fathers de Aguilar and Castanarez; the latter subsequently preached to the Borillos, and after them to the tribe of the Mataguayos, among whom he was treacherously massacred on the 16th of September 1744.

In the yet more southern parts of America other Fathers of the Society had succeeded admirably both with the wandering tribes of the pampas and the inhabitants of the mountain-range which separates Chili from the province of Patagonia, among whom they had begun to form flourishing reductions, when their labours were again assailed with injurious suspicions, and the story of the gold-mines was once more revived.

This time the rumour came from Portugal; and reaching the ear of the viceroy of Brazil, he, in a fit of almost inconceivable credulity, persuaded his government to exchange a colony it possessed on the east side of La Plata for the seven reductions founded on the banks of the Uruguay. So convinced, indeed, was he of the truth of the story, that he even stipulated that the poor Indians should be removed to another part of the province, in order that he might prosecute his search with less interruption; and the proposition having been accepted by the Spanish government, the Fathers of the Society were themselves intrusted with its execution. Bernard Neydorffert was the one to whom it was more especially confided, a man inexpressibly dear to the neophytes, among whom he had spent the best five-and-thirty years of his missionary life; yet when he assembled the caciques of the several reductions, and explained to them the conditions of the treaty, they resisted to a man, declaring that death was preferable to such an exile, and that force alone should drive them from the beloved homes and haunts of their childhood. To force accordingly recourse was had; and the Jesuits, who sought to pacify the minds of the natives, were blamed alike by both parties; the government attributing to their unwillingness the failure of the negotiation, while the Indians, on their part, totally unable to comprehend the position in which the Fathers were placed, and the motives by which they were actuated, openly declared that for once they believed the Fathers had betrayed them. An army was necessary to enforce the treaty, and the wretched inhabitants were driven from their reductions at the point of the bayonet; but when the Portuguese came to explore the mountains which they had wrested from the broken-hearted savage, they discovered too late the fallacy of their expectations; neither silver nor gold could they find, and they were fain to entreat the Jesuits once more to collect and appease the natives, without the aid of whose labours their recent acquisition would have become a desert. This the Fathers were only too happy to attempt; but the savages, after all that had occurred, were naturally sore and suspicious; and the endeavour to bring the natives back to their old homes had by no means been crowned with entire success. when Charles III. ascended the throne of Spain, and breaking the fatal treaty of exchange, to which he had always been opposed, resumed the Uruguay reductions as a portion of his own dominions, in the year 1759, just nine years after the separation.

But the time was fast approaching when the reductions of South America were to exist no more except in the history of the country which had cradled them, and of the Society which had given them birth, and whose name will through all times be identified with theirs. Henceforth, indeed, the Jesuits were to be severed finally and for ever from those missions which they had founded with so much pain and toil, and had cemented with their blood; and which, deprived of their vigilant and careful guardianship, were too soon to lose their distinctive character as the home of the civilised Indian, and to dwindle, under the ignorance and oppression of those by whom the charge had been usurped, into mere aggregations of half-Christian half-heathen, partially reclaimed, but wholly helpless and untaught barbarians. It is true that the Fathers had been pronounced innocent by the king's own appointed judges,—that they had been proved innocent by the bootless search of the Portuguese for gold in their reductions,—that they had proved themselves innocent by their calm submission to the government at a moment when, by countenancing the revolt of their neophytes, they might have opposed violence to injustice, and have changed into substantial reality the kingdom they were accused of coveting in the new world:—innocent, then, they were, if innocence can be established by any amount of testimony; innocent of any designs against the state, of any unlawful lust for riches or for power in the formation and conduct of their reductions. But the principle with which they had inaugurated their work in the beginning was that which wrought its downfall in the end; for in advocating the personal freedom of the native as the basis of their system for his regeneration, they were demanding the one sole boon which the colonists were determined to withhold. It was a *principle*, however, and therefore not to be relinquished, whatever might be the cost to its upholders; but precisely because it was a principle, and not a mere opinion, it had been ever urged by the Society, firmly indeed and earnestly, and with unwearied energy and perseverance, but without any unseemly ebullition of passion or ill-will towards its antagonists; and, content themselves to oppose facts to falsehood, we ever find its members, throughout the turbulent history of those first colonial governments, and all the temptations presented to ill-regulated ambition, on the side of justice, order, and religion. Thus, while the Jesuit dared boldly to reprove and withstand the Spaniards in their ill-usage of the native, he never hesitated to risk his own life to avert from them the merited vengeance of the irritated savage; and while persecution, calumny, and intrigue were still darkening around him, he pursued his missionary career silently, grandly, and heroically, and with the martyr's blood and the martyr's palm replied to the senseless outcries of his accusers. But neither patient endurance nor active deeds of charity and goodness could silence a burst of hatred which was the result of passion and not of reason; and while the Jesuits were shedding their blood in the new world with a profusion that would have been reckless if the cause had been less noble, every nation in the old was ringing with the accusations of their traducers; and every court in Europe contained implacable and powerful foes, who had definitely vowed their downfall.

Into the particulars of the cabal by which their ruin was accomplished at Madrid we have here no need to enter, our only object being to treat of the effect of its machinations upon the reductions. It will be sufficient, therefore, to say, that the mind of the king was gradually and systematically poisoned against them; that he was taught to distrust their intentions, and, jealous as he was of his royal prerogative, to tremble at their power. According to Schœl, Adam, and other Protestant historians, a letter attacking his legitimacy, and, of course, his right to the crown, purporting to be written by the general of the Jesuits, but in reality forged by their arch-enemy the Duke de Choiseul, set the seal upon his resentment, and enabled Aranda, his prime-minister and their worst foe, to obtain from him that final act by which they were banished from his dominions. The reductions were of course included in this sweeping sentence. The decree was signed on the 27th of March 1767; and the war-ship, which brought directions for its secret and speedy execution, cast anchor in the Plata on the 7th of June 1767. On the 21st of the next month, sealed orders to this effect were deposited with all the under-governors of the vice-regal province; and on the 22d its provisions were fully and effectually carried out, the Fathers being seized, every one at his own reduction, and sent off prisoners to Buenos Ayres. The mandate was positive, containing neither exception nor discretionary power; and not one was left behind;—young and old, sick and dying, all at one fell swoop being hurried away from the land to which they had consecrated their labours and their lives, and in which they had humbly hoped to find a grave, amid the prayers and blessings of the savages whom they had reclaimed. Bucareli, the viceroy of Buenos Ayres, was in the province with a body of chosen troops; but the precaution was not needed. The Jesuits had often indeed, and fearlessly, opposed the Spaniards when they oppressed their Indians; but now that the injustice was only against themselves, not an opposing voice was heard among them; the order for their expulsion was obeyed without a murmur, and in many places it was no sooner signified to the Father of the mission than he surrendered himself, on the instant, without even the appearance of compulsion being necessary for his removal. Yet it cannot be doubted, that had they chosen to appeal to their neophytes, the argument of force and numbers would have been strongly in their favour; and that they did not do so was, therefore, their last and most conclusive answer to their accusers,—their last and most effective protest against that voice from Europe which declared that "the aggrandisement of their own society was the sole object of its members."

The exiled Fathers were shipped for Italy, where they subsisted on a pittance doled out by the Spanish government; subject, however, to the condition, that they should neither speak nor write in defence of their society; and to this tyrannical exaction was superadded another still more insulting, namely, that the transgression of a single member in this particular should be imputed to the entire body, and punished accordingly.

They were replaced in most of their deserted missions by a mongrel government, consisting half of ecclesiastics and half of laymen; but called as they were to the task without tact, experience, or knowledge of the peculiarities of the people with whom they had to deal, the attempt is on all sides acknowledged to have been a failure. Hardly, indeed, could it have been otherwise; for though the Indians had received deep religious impressions, and had made rapid strides towards the order and industry of civilised life, yet the lawless habits of centuries to a certain extent still hung about them; and they could not be kept together as a social body without a very nice and judicious adjustment of the influences that were brought to bear upon them. In this adjustment the government of the Jesuits had been as eminently successful as that of their successors was confessedly otherwise; the former possessing in its rule a unity of purpose which commanded the respect of the Indians, while the latter, being ever and always divided against itself, left the unhappy objects of its jurisdiction either perplexed as to the authority to be obeyed, or doubtful altogether of the necessity of obedience. The lay governor was most frequently a tyrant, and whereas the Jesuits had done all on system, every thing thereafter was unsettled and uncertain; individual caprice being substituted for a code of regulations which had given consistency to punishment and dignity to justice, and fear being everywhere employed to compel submission where before kindness had been the only prevailing argument. Such a government, and so directed, soon told with fatal effect upon the reductions; and although less than a century has elapsed since they were first subjected to its influence, it has nearly succeeded in effacing all of mental cultivation and external beauty which the Jesuits had effected in their missions. Little but desolation is now to be seen, where once the Jesuit's house and the Indian's cottage stood in peaceful prosperity side by side. The public buildings have disappeared; the churches are all in ruins; the cottages have degenerated into native wigwams; briers and weeds everywhere complete the picture of decay; the population has dwindled from thousands to hundreds, and such as still remain have half resumed the indolence of the savage, and stand listless, desolate, and sad, at the doors of their poverty-stricken dwellings; while in reductions which once could pay without personal privation, though not without wholesome labor, a yearly tribute to the king, the superior of the missions can hardly find wherewithal to keep starvation from his people.

That the condition of the South-American Indian at the present day would have been far different to what it is, had the Jesuits been suffered to finish the work they had begun so well, it will be hardly possible to doubt, if we judge by what they did of what they would have done; and this seems, after all, the only fair and equitable way of trying the question. For eighty years they held possession of the land; and in those eighty years, out of hundreds of wandering tribes, separated from each other by habits, language, religion, and the natural animosity that arms savage against savage, they succeeded in forming a nation one in habits, language, government,—above all, one in Christian and fraternal unity; impressing on all so deep and broad a mark of civilisation, that the traces are visible even to this hour. The Guarani Indians, whom at so much cost and trouble they brought to habits of industry and order, still hold together as a Christian people, and still constitute the bulk of the working population; so that whatever of agricultural skill is brought to bear upon the land is the result entirely of the old reductions. The Guarani language also retains the pre-eminence which the Jesuits gave it, and is still the only organ of communication among the inhabitants of Paraguay. Nor is the missionary himself forgotten, although two generations have passed away since he was seen in the land. His name is still blest by those who hear it, and his return still looked for as an era of good fortune in the future of the native Indian. Even many of the little religious customs which he taught his neophytes still linger among their descendants. "To this day," says a recent traveller, "the children in Paraguay never retire to rest without kneeling to ask the blessing of their parents; and the parents, in reply to the question of the stranger, will tell him that the good Jesuit Fathers instructed them to do so."

When we consider the men by whom those Fathers were replaced, and the sort of government which was substituted for their paternal rule, we shall wonder rather that so much has been retained than that so much has been swept away. It is not in eighty years that the most wisely-conceived and most efficiently-applied system of cultivation can be indelibly impressed upon the character of a nation. A thorough civilisation is the growth of centuries; and although that which has been more suddenly developed may seem to flourish for a time under the stimulus of authority, it is almost certain eventually to fail. It is fatal to the very body of the savage, which perishes beneath its unaccustomed softnesses; as a mountain-flower might fade if exposed unadvisedly to the atmosphere of a hot-house. It dwarfs the very powers of the mind it is intended to enlarge, by coming too suddenly upon it before it has been duly prepared for its reception; and it either ceases entirely the moment the forcing influence has been withdrawn, or it merely freezes the surface of society into a factitious smoothness, while all the normal vices of the barbarian run darkly in the tide below. Savage nations are, in fact, as little fitted to receive at once the full measure of civilisation, pressed down and running over, as an infant to take upon himself the duties of a man; and if the child requires to be instructed day by day in the mysteries of existence, so a rude untutored people must needs be led, generation after generation, into the full light of social knowledge —which to us, indeed, is a second nature, because it is our inheritance from our ancestors, but which, we must not forget, those ancestors won step by step, and were centuries in acquiring. Both nature and experience, then, point to the principle of gradual initiation as the only safe one in the instruction of savage nations; and therefore Raynal himself, the utterer of so many blasphemies against the Catholic religion, has yet not hesitated to declare, in his *Political and Philosophical History of the Indies*, that " when the Jesuits were taken from the reductions, their Indians had arrived at the highest point of civilisation to which it perhaps is possible to conduct new nations, and to one certainly far higher than any other people of the new world had hitherto been brought. In them the laws were every where regularly carried out; manners were pure; a happy spirit of fraternity united all hearts; the useful arts were carried to perfection; while those which were merely ornamental were cultivated with some success."

Most unjustly, then, it follows, have the Jesuits been reproached, as if they kept the Indian purposely in the tutelage of a child, when in fact they were only fitting him in the best and most effective manner for the full use and benefit of that freedom which, by their own unprompted and unselfish efforts, they had won him from his foes. In the beginning, indeed, all the business of the reductions passed of necessity through their hands; but the work was gradually and almost imperceptibly transferred to the children of their early converts, who, born in the bosom of a civilised Christianity, were easily instructed in many things which their fathers, the painted warriors and hunters just taken from the woods, could never have been brought to comprehend. In the latter days of the reductions, all the mercantile transactions of the mission—the exchange of goods, and arrangement of the tribute, as well as the providing for the various necessities of the inhabitants,—no light task for any brain—were confided to men whose forefathers, only two generations before, had been so ignorant of numbers, that four was the highest figure they could count without the assistance of their fingers. And be it remembered, that all this was effected amidst difficulties more numerous and more perplexing than perhaps any similar enterprise had ever presented; for not only had the missionaries to contend with the prejudices of the nations to whom they were sent to preach, but to encounter the unceasing hostility of the people in whose company they came; and it was amidst every opposition which the upholders of the slave-trade could bring to bear against them, that they introduced the Indians into the fold of Christ, and to all the blessings and virtues of civilised society and domestic life. Long ago they had promised the Spaniards to make men and Christians of the savages and cannibals of whom they were sent in search:—brave promise it was indeed, yet not a rash one; for who shall say that it was not fulfilled to the very letter in the reductions of Paraguay, which Voltaire himself pronounced to be the "triumph of humanity!"

THE END